Sexual Aliveness

Also by Edward W. L. Smith, Ph.D.
The Body in Psychotherapy (McFarland, 1985)
The Growing Edge of Gestalt Therapy (edited)

Sexual Aliveness

by
Edward W. L. Smith

McFarland & Company, Inc., Publishers
Jefferson, North Carolina, and London

Library of Congress Cataloguing-in-Publication Data

Smith, Edward W. L., 1942–
  Sexual aliveness.

  Bibliography: p. 115
  1. Psychosexual disorders.   2. Sex (Psychology)
3. Gestalt therapy. 4. Reich, Wilhelm, 1897–1957.
I. Title.
RC556.S65   1987   616.85′83   87-42521

ISBN 0-89950-268-7 (acid-free natural paper)

Manufactured in the United States of America.

McFarland   Box 611   Jefferson NC 28640

*The worst of sexual perversions
is celibacy. — Roger W. Wescott*

Table of Contents

List of Figures

Preface

With the bookshelves replete with offerings on various aspects of sexuality, why write yet another book on sex? I have asked myself this question several times, and each time I have found the same reply. I believe that I have something worthwhile to say. Much of it may be found here and there in the already existing literature. But my form for conveying what I have to say is mine. I am offering here a particular configuration concerning sexuality. It will, I hope, prove to be fresh, interesting, exciting, persuasive, and instructional.

As a psychotherapist I spend many hours a week with unhappy people. Some feel troubled, some feel dull. In either case, agitated or bored, and regardless of the specific symptomatic feelings and behaviors, these people are not experiencing the degree of richness, meaningfulness, and satisfaction that they want and which is possible. At the most abstract level, then, I see my job as that of a facilitator in their creating a way of living which is rich, meaningful, and satisfying. At the next level, one step less abstract, my job is to facilitate aliveness in the persons with whom I work.

As I see it, richness, meaningfulness, and satisfaction ensue when a path of aliveness is followed. That is not to say that there are not natural and even inevitable discomforts, frustrations, and pains. These, too, are part of being alive, and they, too, contribute to the satisfaction of a meaningful life, lived richly.

This book is about sexual aliveness. I believe that being alive and being sexual are at one level synonymous. And so I explore what it means to be sexually alive and how the natural rhythms of sex can be viewed. I then look at the why and how of sexual deadening, the creation of sexual dysfunctions. Next, I explore the arena of sexual perversion, those ways of maintaining sexual aliveness which take unnatural and problematic forms. And, finally, I address some of the philosophical issues — political and moral — which form the cultural context for sexual aliveness.

1. Being Sexually Alive

The idea that aliveness and sexuality are close companions is one which has been discussed by many writers in psychology, among them Alexander Lowen, Fritz Perls, and their mentor Wilhelm Reich. The boldest and most succinct statement is that of Lowen (1980, p. 19), "To be sexual is to be alive, and to be alive is to be sexual." Appealing in its simplicity, this equation deserves careful exploration. By itself the equation is but the tip of the iceberg, or perhaps more aptly the cone of the volcano. Let us explore the undergirding, the larger context beginning with the most obvious level of sexuality — genitality.

The genital level of sexual aliveness has to do with relating *to* one's genitals and to other people *through* one's genitals. So, the genital level of sexuality is what is usually implied by the terms "being sexual" and "sexual relationship." We are exploring here two arenas of genital sexuality, that of self-relating and that of relating to others.

By now there seems to be consensus among educated societies that relating to one's own genitals is natural and does not carry the

1

threat of catastrophe which was once widely believed. Ideas such as that masturbation causes blindness or insanity seem laughable. And rarely, except in jest, do educated people talk of "self-abuse" or of the "solitary vice." The history of antimasturbation is, however, a long one, and one carried forth by people of respect and distinction. Among these are Benjamin Rush, Esquirol, Krafft-Ebing, Karl Meninger, and even Freud. In their writings one can find support for the "doctrine of masturbatory insanity" (Szasz, 1980). The current situation is an inversion of the old belief, as Szasz (1980, p. 64) has so nicely stated: "In the nineteenth century, masturbating was an illness and not masturbating was a treatment; today, not masturbating is a disease and masturbating is a treatment." It seems that there is no harm in masturbation *per se.* The only harm is that which comes from guilt over the autoerotic act.

So, what is masturbation? It is what one does to oneself to bring about genital pleasure. It is relating to one's own genitals. It appears that almost everyone does masturbate. The frequency and style of one's masturbation is, of course, a reflection of that person's broader way of being-in-the-world. In other words, personality is reflected in one's masturbatory style. One's aliveness, one's position for living may be apparent in how shy or bold one is in masturbating, how routinized or inventive, and how serious or how playful. Offit (1981, p. 173) has stated that "People who do not masturbate are frequently unable not only to touch themselves but also to enjoy life's other satisfactions. For them, pleasure is often understood as sin."

One of the synonyms for masturbation, autoeroticism, calls attention to the essential quality of attention being directed to one's self. This is, in Gestalt therapy terminology, a retroflection. Retroflection means to turn the focus of expression back on one's self, to make one's self the target of one's action. Retroflection is reflexive, and is often identified by the presence of a reflexive pronoun. For example, I may describe my autoeroticism as "giving pleasure to *myself*" or "making love to *myself*." The essential quality here is that the interaction is entirely contained by one person. In other words I interact with myself, being both the "doer" and the "done to."

So, in masturbation there is a retroflection of interaction. Retroflection of interaction is of two kinds. The distinction is subtle, but nevertheless important. First, retroflected interaction may be *doing to myself what I would like to do to you.* In the second case, retroflected interaction is *doing to myself what I would like for you to do to me.* Think of manual masturbation to clarify this distinction. In the hand-genital contact there can be genital action directed toward the hand, or there can be hand action directed toward the genitals. Even if the masturbatory style involves both, the two elements remain. The parallel in sexual intercourse is clear. I can be active and you can be passive. You can make love to me. Or, we can both be active. We can make love to each other. And so, too, in masturbation; I can make love to me, or be made love to, by me, or both.

A negative bias toward masturbation could be read into the above. This is not, however, what I want to convey. As I view it, masturbation is, in a positive sense, a substitute for interpersonal genital sex. It is a retroflected interaction as I described above, but that does not mean that it is inferior *per se.* If one wants to beget children, then masturbation is not appropriate, obviously. Furthermore, masturbation does not provide for the interaction of two human energy fields with all the richness which can come from that. So, in terms of these two ends, masturbation is not inferior, it is just not appropriate. There are circumstances, however, in which autoeroticism is the genital activity of choice.

Masturbation is an avenue of self-exploration as well as self-knowing. (The double meaning of "self-knowing" is apt.) It allows a marvelous sexual self-sufficiency. One can attend the sexual urge without the cooperation of another. Perhaps this is the greatest value of masturbation. It does ease the sometimes heavy burden and complications of human interdependencies. So, for all of the wonder, richness, and beauty which sexual relationships can bring, masturbation provides an avenue of sexual release free from the complication of relationships.

And, too, masturbation is safe. One can be autoerotic without risk of venereal disease, rejection, unwanted pregnancy, or personal harm. When the risk of these is too great, masturbation may be the sexual outlet of choice. And when an appropriate sexual partner is not available, masturbation is. Masturbation is one's own, private business. And surely, whether one wants to share one's genital aliveness or not is one's own choice.

Masturbation, as I see it, has an important role in one's life profile. Sexual aliveness most likely will involve some autoerotic activities. Boredom, loneliness, work stress, tiredness, insomnia, and rejection all seem to be ameliorated by masturbation, as well as sexual tension itself. There are many times when these conditions arise, but an appropriate sex partner is not available.

Mark Twain put it well in a satirical address of 1879 (Szasz, 1980, p. 62):

> To the lonely it is company; to the forsaken it is a friend; to the aged and to the impotent it is a benefactor; they that are pennyless are yet rich, in that they still have this majestic diversion.

Masturbation, although most often thought of as a private and solitary form of sexuality, has a potential role in sexual relationships. "Dual masturbation," or masturbation in the presence of each other, may serve the function of desensitization of anxiety which one or both of the partners may feel about being interpersonal with their sexuality. This can be an easier, intermediate step between solitary masturbation and sex with a partner. To masturbate in another's presence is to share an intimacy, and yet keep in control of the activity. In "mutual masturbation" the next step is taken wherein each of the partners "masturbates" the other, either taking turns or doing so simultaneously. I find this a confused term, used in the literature (for example *The Encyclopedia of Sexual Behavior*, 1961). The confusion is that masturbation *qua* autoeroticism is just that, self provided. Descriptively, mutual masturbation is manual stimulation of the partner's genitals. This may serve as foreplay, leading to genital-genital contact, or it may be continued to orgasm. In either case it may serve as a form of genital contact more comfortable for that moment than genital to genital contact.

I want to move now to the second arena of genital sexuality, that of relating to another.

There is the necessity, if humankind is to continue, that some people relate sexually in a specific manner. The penis-vagina relationship is a biological necessity. That is not to say that *everyone* must engage in penis-vagina intercourse. Nor is it to say that *anyone* must limit her or his genital activity with others to the one penis–one vagina format. The necessity is that some people at the biologically appropriate time relate penis to vagina. This is an existential given, part of the condition of being a human animal. Even though there has been far-reaching speculation about futuristic alternatives to reproduction through heterosexual intercourse, and successful experimentation with artificial insemination, the fact remains that heterosexual intercourse is the natural process for human life to beget human life. Aldous Huxley's *Brave New World* notwithstanding, the time-honored method prevails.

Human sexuality is based in biology. Part of the natural condition of being human is to have the sexual urge. The sexual urge involves the wanting to penetrate or to be penetrated. With the waxing and waning of the sexual urge, as the hormones undergo their cycles, people move toward and away from sexual contacts.

But human sexuality is also based in emotions. Not only does the human condition carry the sexual urge, but also the sexual feelings of love and lust. Love contains the experiences of tenderness, caring, respecting, and cherishing. These blend with lust, or the passion of attraction, to constitute the emotion of sexual love. So, genital sexuality is not only in the service of our biological need, but also in the service of our emotional expression. Put simply, and so simple it is as to be a truism, people can have sex for the purpose of procreation, but more often have sex as an expression of their feelings of love and lust.

With the recognition of the legitimacy of having sex for emotional reasons, and not just to fulfill the biological necessity of procreation, there is a wider possibility for genital activities. No longer is the penis-vagina connection the only satisfying mode. The possibility can be considered of other combinations such as genital-mouth, genital-anus, genital-hand. With procreation as the goal, the format is narrowly dictated, but when the goal becomes the pleasure of emotional fulfillment, the format for genital relating becomes wide. These other formats are variations on the basic one, and only the basic penis-vagina format allows for both the biological and emotional ends to be attended. But when the biological end is not important, or even not wanted, other genital formats gain in importance. Not only do they allow emotional fulfillment without the risk of pregnancy, but they provide variety. And variety is the most consistently effective aphrodisiac.

Being sexually alive involves some relating through one's genitals. This means relating to at least someone through one's genitals, sometimes. Beyond the decision to be sexual there is a major choice point which has to do with the blend of love and lust that one experiences. If the blend is highly weighted toward love, with lust lacking, genital activity will be diminished and in the extreme the relationship is platonic. Conversely, with lust running high and love weak or absent, there will be more impersonal sex. The extreme is recreational sex, wherein the partner's identity becomes nearly irrelevant. This dimension is dealt with nicely by Stanley Keleman (1982, p. 96), "We can choose to make sex impersonal, to permit sexuality to exist simply as a mechanism for pleasure . . . or we can choose to see sexuality as an act of love, accompanied by the formation of emotional bonds and the evolution of our humanness through the life of relationships . . . "

So, the question of sexual aliveness is both one of quantity and quality. In terms of quantity, the question is how *sexually active* is the person. Each person is her or his best judge of the level of sexual activity which is best. The issue of quality gets to how *sexually satisfied* the person is. I believe it is important to distinguish between sexual activity and sexual satisfaction. At times people tend to confuse the two and think the more sex the better.

What is important in being sexually alive is relating through one's genitals in a manner that brings richness and satisfaction. Mature opinion seems clear that sex as an act of love is far richer than as an act of recreation. I believe that a sexually alive person will tend toward sex as an act of love, as a way of relating, and as a way to build an emotional bond. That means that a high level of sexual activity will not be mistaken for a high level of sexual satisfaction. Also, the sexually alive will be able to experience an emotional blend of love and lust, such that he or she will relate to someone *through* her or his genitals. This contrasts with relationships without genitals and genitals without personal relationships.

Another topic which deserves attention within the realm of genital sexual aliveness is the orgasm itself. It was Wilhelm Reich (1980) who emphasized the distinction between "erective potency" and "orgasmic potency." The distinction, as I see it, applies to women as well as to men; it is just that the man's erection or nonerection is so obvious. So, in the case of either men or women the distinction is between sexual arousal (penile erection or engorgement and lubrication of the vulva) and release of sexual excitement. Traditionally, of course, the issue of "potency," or in Reich's term, "erective potency," has been seen as a male issue exclusively. So much so, in fact, that even the term for lack of genital arousal — "impotent" — has meant an inability to obtain or maintain for an appropriate length of time an erection of the penis. The emphasis on the man is surely at least in part because a man cannot have intercourse without an erection. A woman, on the other hand, can do so with the aid of a foreign lubricant. Our anatomical destiny is that in heterosexual intercourse it is the man who enters the woman and the woman who receives the man.

Reich's distinction between erective potency and orgastic potency relates to the distinction which I drew above, between sexual activity and sexual satisfaction. Sexual activity requires erective potency for the male, whereas sexual satisfaction implies orgastic potency in the case of males and females. The real issue in sexual aliveness is that of satisfaction. So it may be that someone is sexually very active, but finds that satisfaction eludes her or him. By logical implication, a man who is highly active sexually will have a high degree of erective potency. Satisfaction, however, will depend on orgastic potency. Where orgastic potency is low or lacking, and therefore sexual satisfaction is not experienced, unusually high levels of sexual activity may be found. It makes sense that where satisfaction is elusive, a frenetic search is undertaken.

Reich's (1980, p. 18) position is clear and extreme concerning the importance of orgastic potency: "Orgastic potency is to be understood as the ability to achieve full resolution of existing sexual need tension, an ability that is seldom impaired in healthy individuals. It is lacking in neurotics." This stated relationship between the lack of orgastic potency and more general personality dysfunction is one which Reich (1973, 1980) explored extensively, and for which he has presented considerable clinical evidence. His conclusion he stated as follows, " ... there is no neurosis or psychosis without disturbances of the genital function (Reich, 1980, p. 39)." The most meaningful genital dysfunction is, in Reich's view, the dysfunction of orgasm. And, any sexual dysfunction would reflect in the orgasm.

It is often difficult to evaluate one's own or another's orgastic potency. In the case of a woman, if a full orgasm has not ever been experienced, then the woman may not realize that the sensations she does experience in sex are not that. She may feel very pleasant sensations and enjoy the sexual experience very much, and yet not be aware that her orgasm is weak or marginal. If she doesn't feel *any* resolution of sexual tension, of course, then it is obvious that orgasm has not been a part of her sexual encounter. In the man's case, there is also opportunity for misunderstanding the experience of orgasm. This is because male orgasm has been equated by most people with ejaculation. So a simple criterion has been applied to the man. If he ejaculates, he is orgastic; if he doesn't ejaculate he is not orgastic. The evidence that the equation ejaculation = orgasm is oversimplified is that a man may ejaculate and still experience unresolved sexual tension. In both men and women, the lack of satisfaction following a sexual encounter may well indicate low orgastic potency in that instance. Even more cogent evidence of low orgastic potency comes from one's experiencing orgasm, and later, after having experienced full orgasm, realizing that what had been taken for a full orgasm previously was, indeed not.

Reich (1980) has offered some hallmarks by which a high level of orgastic potency can be recognized. First, with full orgasm there is a complete dissipation of sexual excitement. In other words, no residual sexual tension is experienced following the sex act. This criterion brings up an interesting and somewhat controversial point. If full orgasm means a complete dissipation of sexual excitation with no residual tension, then what is the implication for sequential orgasms? Does this mean that the person who wants more than one orgasm is not fully orgastically potent? The answer, I believe, is too complex to be given justice merely by a "yes" or "no."

There are different routes to the desire for sequential orgasms. If a person has a weak orgasm in the presence of high sexual excitement, then there will be residual sexual tension. This person may need several orgasms to process the sexual energy, and even then, if capable only of weak orgasms, may be left with a degree of unsatisfied sexual urge. The extreme situation is represented by the person who has many and frequent orgasms, yet still feels sexually unsatisfied. In this case there is reason to suspect that orgastic potency may be low.

Keep in mind also that a verbal report of "good orgasms" may not be an accurate portrayal of the phenomenon in question. A person who has not experienced a strong, full orgasm may believe that the diminished orgasms which he or she does experience are the ultimate which one can experience. There is much clinical evidence for this point. Patients sometimes report after successful therapy that they are now having orgasms which demonstrate to them that what they previously experienced were very pale versions thereof, or even that what they experienced previously were pleasant sensations which they had mislabeled as orgasms. So, the report of sequential orgasms, or the report of the desire for sequential orgasms, just as much as the report of residual sexual tension following orgasm *may* be evidence for low orgastic potency.

There are conditions under which one's sexual excitement is extremely easily aroused, so that even after a satisfying orgasm and a brief rest one is again feeling a welling up of the sexual urge. One such situation is the availability of a desirable sexual partner following a prolonged period of sexual abstinence. So, the sailor fresh in port after a long voyage or the husband returning from a business trip may find that one orgasm, even if full and satisfying, leaves him and his partner still eager for more. Another situation is that of new lovers. Here, again, the two people may have satisfying orgasms only to find that in a little while they are sexually aroused.

Other examples of such situations could be offered. There is a common element to these situations, and that is novelty. The return to one's partner after a prolonged absence, or the finding of a new partner both provide novelty. And, it seems, novelty is the only aphrodisiac known to be reliable. So, under these conditions in which novelty is created, whether by change of partner, change of circumstance, or even change of setting, there may be a move toward the desire for several orgasms. And this desire may be in the context of high orgastic potency.

The crucial aspect of the criterion of complete dissipation of sexual excitation for orgastic potency is the match between level of excitation and level of potency of the attending orgasm. Put simply, one is orgastically potent when one's orgasm adequately reduces the sexual tension which was experienced. When one is satisfied after sex, one has been orgastically potent. When one is left tense and aroused after sex, one has not been orgastically potent. And, under special circumstances one may want to repeat the cycle of arousal and satisfaction, even though, or perhaps because the result was so satisfying. The criterion is to be applied to one cycle of sex — arousal to satisfaction — not to any particular time period such as an hour, a night, or a weekend. With these understandings, I believe that Reich's criterion is useful.

In passing, I want to draw attention to the distinction between sequential orgasm, discussed above, and multiple orgasm. Sequential orgasm refers to a repeat of the sexual cycle. So, after orgasm there is a rest period of a few minutes and then a rearousal and orgastic resolution. Both men and women are often capable of these sequential orgasms, under those circumstances discussed above. There is, however, a difference between men and women concerning multiple orgasms, that is, two or more orgasms within a matter of minutes. Each of these orgasms may be strong, sometimes each one getting stronger than the ones prior. These orgasms occur without a rest period and rearousal following satisfaction, and in this crucial way distinguish themselves from sequential orgasms.

My guess is that more men experience or could experience multiple orgasms than are aware of it, but fail to recognize this because of equating orgasm with ejaculation. Whereas the man may ejaculate only once without a several minute refractory period, he may be able to experience two or more periods of orgastic spasms before "coming down." There is still some controversy as to what constitutes a "nonterminative minor climax" and what is a "complete orgasm." It does appear, however, that Masters and Johnson have demonstrated the validity of multiple orgasms in women. Who knows how common this is? Many years ago Kinsey reported a figure of 14 percent for the women in his study. The important thing, in terms of sexual aliveness, is orgastic potency. Whether single orgasm or multiple orgasms, the issue is the satisfying resolution of sexual tension.

Returning to the topic of orgastic potency, Reich's second hallmark is a rather rapid transition from the voluntary movements to the involuntary pelvic movements. What this means is that at some point during the voluntarily controlled thrusting movements (this phase being dominated by sensory experience) there will be an involuntary takeover into much more rapid thrusting (this phase being dominated by motor experience). The transition point is very brief when orgastic potency is high. With some styles of having sex one of the partners may remain relatively passive during this first phase. This is often true in oral sex wherein there is an active partner giving sex to a receiving partner.

The receiver, being relatively or totally passive in terms of pelvic movements, tends, then, to have a slower and less energetic shift into the involuntary phase of thrusting. In fact, with oral sex the amount of pelvic thrusting is often greatly diminished throughout the sexual act. Sometimes side to side or wiggling movements are used rather than the rocking back and forth of the pelvis. This may yield pleasurable sensations to both partners, but if maintained to orgasm it will diminish its strength. The orgasm itself involves jerking, spasmodic, forward and backward movements of the pelvis. It is as if the side to side or wiggling motion is a statement of "no," just as shaking the head from side to side conveys. So, either a passive pelvis or a pelvis wiggling side to side will tend to slow down the transition into involuntary thrusting, and if persisted in, will tend to decrease the potency of that orgasm.

A third hallmark of orgastic potency is the ability to focus temporarily all of one's attention and emotion on the genital experience, despite conflicts in one's life. This means that one is able to be fully in the here-and-now of the sexual experience. Rather than wandering away to another place or time in one's fantasy, or feeling emotions which belong to another place and time, one stays in the immediate and actual experience of the sexual activity, and increasingly so as orgasm is approached. As sexual foreplay begins, one's attention may be split between the moment and activity at hand and some other concern. But as sex progresses, the other concerns need to fade into background allowing sex to be the figure of attention. This means that troubles and conflicts are put aside as one focuses more and more completely on sex. By the time one approaches the threshold of orgasm and crosses, all attention is on the immediate experience. Everything but the orgastic experience is swept away when orgastic potency is high.

This brings up the controversy about the role of fantasy in sex. I believe there is a fairly simple guideline which makes fantasy non-controversial, except of course on moral grounds. I am not intending to deal here with the moral issues of having sexual fantasies, such as the rightness or wrongness of imagining someone else's spouse while making love to one's own. Rather, I want to look at the role of fantasy in contributing or distracting from sexual aliveness. I wrote earlier in this chapter about novelty as an aphrodisiac. Fantasy is a wondrously effective way of bringing novelty to bear on one's sex life. One can fantasize all sorts of locations, circumstances, and partners and thus enjoy the sexually stimulating effects of fantasy without the real dangers inherent if those fantasies were enacted in reality. I see sexual fantasy as a rich source of stimulation to arousal. This is the contribution of fantasy to one's sexuality — its arousal function. My suggested guideline, then, is that to the extent that fantasy contributes to one's desired sexual arousal, it is of value.

So, fantasy which is attuned to one's sexual experience may enhance that experience. On the other hand, fantasy which is at variance with one's experience may distract and diminish that experience. In the latter case, the fantasy may be taking one away from what is immediate and available, splitting one's attention, with the result being a decrease in arousal. As the sexual experience progresses toward orgasm the value of fantasy decreases. For arousal, fantasy may enhance, but for the intense physical sensations which occur in orgasm and as one approaches orgasm, fantasy may actually be a deterrent. Fantasy fades as one becomes highly involved in the takeover of involuntary thrusting and the intense, high energy, pleasurable physical sensations.

A problem can be created by misuse of sexual fantasy as I have pointed out. I want to describe a specific circumstance which can be problematic. One may have an ideal lover in one's fantasy. When one has sex with one's literal partner, in fantasy he or she is making love with the ideal lover. This can develop a strong bond between the person and the ideal lover, a bond of love and erotic attachment. This bond may be as strong as that between two literal lovers. The problem is when those feelings of love and lust are not transferred onto the literal partner. If this transfer of feelings does not occur, then the literal partner, not being the ideal of one's dreams, seems second best. The result can be a sense of fraud, that what one got was not the best, not what one really wanted. If the transference is made from the ideal partner to one's literal partner during the sexual experience, then one is likely to feel satisfied. But, if that transference is not made, there will likely be a feeling of disappointment and lack of satisfaction following intercourse. Without the transference from the ideal lover of one's fantasy to the actual lover, there is a maintaining of an illusion. The more powerful the illusion, the less satisfaction with one's actual partner.

I have seen this problem operating with patients. One particularly interesting instance of this problem is when someone's partner has ended the relationship, leaving that person sad and feeling rejected. A way of maintaining the illusion of still being connected with the rejecting lover is to fantasize being with that lover while masturbating or while having sex with someone else. To some, this is a way of hanging on to the old relationship. The illusion, kept alive through sexual fantasy, is a way to avoid some of the pain of grieving the dead relationship. I was curious about the length of time a patient of mine was taking in grieving the loss of her lover. She seemed to me to be doing the mourning labor well, and yet the period of grief seemed to me protracted. On a hunch I asked her about her sexual fantasies. What she revealed was that she almost always had fantasies of her ex-lover making love to her while she masturbated. With this, we recognized, she had kept her illusions alive and delayed the acceptance of his being gone.

So, we see, sexual fantasies can be used to benefit sexual arousal or to the detriment of sexual satisfaction.

In summary, Reich (1980) offered three hallmarks of orgastic potency. First, a complete dissipation of sexual tension following orgasm. Second, a rapid transition during sex from the slow, voluntary pelvic movements to the fast, involuntary pelvic movements. And third, the ability to focus temporarily all of one's attention on the genital experience, regardless of the emotional conflicts in one's life. At those times when these conditions prevail, one is orgastically potent. One's orgastic potency may diminish at times, as evidenced by a failure in one or more of these criteria.

I want to consider next the choice of not being sexually active for an extended period of time. The terms which may be used for this, interchangeably, are sexual abstinence, celibacy, and chastity. In the context of sexual aliveness, what, then, is the meaning of celibacy?

An extreme position has been taken by some people such as Roger Wescott, who has said "The worst of sexual perversions is celibacy." Similarly, Aldous Huxley wrote in *Eyeless in Gaza*, "Chastity — the most unnatural of the sexual perversions." The position taken therein is that to be sexual is natural. Sexual expression may be perverted, but the most perverse form of all is not to engage in sex of any form. Not to be sexual is unnatural.

At the very least, to be celibate is to live "as if" one had no genitals. Not to be sexual means to live without experiencing an arena which is natural, emotionally rich, and undeniably power- ful. So, one's possible wholeness is not lived out in celibacy. On the physical level one regards oneself in the same manner as one of those statues or drawings in which the genital area is barren. Physical wholeness is denied. Behaviorally, too, there is a lack of wholeness, as such a potentially rich arena of human activity is omitted.

To give up one's sexuality would seem to require very strong motivation either in the form of sacrificing it for some great reward or avoiding it out of strong fear. More is understood, I believe, about the latter motivation. The notion that sexual abstinence could spring from a fear of sexuality has a common-sense validity. In addition, the psychoanalytic literature provides both theoretical discussions and clinical examples of this dynamic. Reich (1980) has stated that he found that men usually cite a fear of impotence as the reason for their abstinence, when seen in a clinical setting. He went on to demonstrate a close relation between male impotence and "sexual timidity" in women. Reich's position is clearly that most celibacy is neurotically based.

But what of celibacy for religious reasons? Here it is necessary to distinguish two levels of religiously based celibacy. First is sexual abstinence outside marriage. Second is sexual abstinence for the purpose of attaining spiritual enlightenment or higher states of consciousness. Both of these religiously based reasons for sexual abstinence are valid at the socio-political-spiritual level. As such, there can be a very strong motivation for celibacy.

No doubt there are many instances in which a religious motivation is claimed for one's celibacy, when this claim is a cover to avoid facing with others or even with oneself the fear of sexuality.

If one has strong fears of sexuality, or if one has difficulty in relating to others because of poor social skills, religious ideology can serve as a socially acceptable excuse for sexual abstinence.

Interestingly, Reich (1980, p. 116) has reported from clinical experience that "Ideologically approved abstinence of long duration must be viewed as a special form of impotence, because experience shows that when individuals decide to have intercourse after a long period of abstinence, genital disorders sooner or later emerge." He is suggesting, I believe, that religiously approved celibacy can be equated with impotence of a type. His evidence is that the genital function does not emerge and remain intact following the lifting of the celibacy. This is not to say that impotence necessarily led to the choice of sexual abstinence, however. That is one possibility; another is that the prolonged abstinence resulted in a genital dysfunction.

Zilbergeld (1978), in *Male Sexuality*, has suggested a number of reasons for celibacy. He mentions preoccupation with an engrossing, extended project, lack of sexual interest or energy, "deep depression," times when sex would get in the way of important processes or decisions, and times for getting to know oneself better. His approach is to offer support to people who believe that a period of sexual abstinence would be useful, for any of these reasons mentioned. What Zilbergeld has presented leaves room for clarification. Certainly, one's sexual rhythms are affected by much of what is going on in one's life. So, it may well be that while working on a big project one would have less time and interest for sexual activity. But, why celibacy? If one is "deeply depressed," of course, there will be low libido. But the lack of sexual interest during depression or any other extended time may well be recognized as a symptom of an underlying process which is not normal. (Zilbergeld fails to distinguish "depression" as a pathological process and "grieving," which is the natural process of coming to terms with an important loss. During the grieving process there are periods during which libido is also low.) Sex can be used as a distraction, an escape from unpleasant realities which need to be faced and dealt with. If one is using sex in that way, then it would be useful to stop doing that. But, again, is celibacy necessary? Of the several reasons which Zilbergeld suggests for sexual abstinence, the only one which seems neither to be based on a pathological condition nor to be overstated in its appropriateness is self-exploration.

It is not always easy to recognize the neurotic reasons for celibacy. The stated reasons often sound quite credible. Examples include lack of opportunity, lack of money for dating, lack of time because of being too busy with other things, or not finding the right person. If such reasons are used chronically, it is appropriate to suspect an underlying fear. Some other reasons for sexual abstinence sound even more convincing. As mentioned above, a stated religious reason may be given which is in fact a cover for fears about sexuality. Fear of venereal disease may also serve that function; it may seem like a credible reason for sexual abstinence, and under certain circumstances certainly is a wise choice. But, again, that stated reason can be used as an avoidance of encountering one's sexuality.

The next question is whether sexual abstinence by itself has harmful effects. In the above discussion celibacy has been taken to mean abstinence from sex with another, but not to include a refraining from masturbation. To address the question of harmful effects of celibacy I will shift to a meaning of total abstinence. Total abstinence, the excluding of all forms of direct sexual satisfaction is probably quite rare. But what about a sexually mature person who abstains for an extended period of time? Reich (1973, 1980) was very clear in his statements of the importance of orgasm in the economic management of life energy. Without orgasm, he believed, there will accumulate a stasis of energy which can lead to physiological as well as psychological problems. His position predicts harmful effects in the case of long term sexual abstinence.

Eva Reich once told me that her father said that if you go without sex for three months you will go crazy. Reich (1980) stated that the fate of genital libido in abstinent individuals who appear to be healthy is unclear, somewhat of a mystery. His reasoning is as follows. Even though degree of libido and the rhythm of the need for release of sexual tension shows great variation from person to person, the sexual apparatus has not stopped functioning. Except in the individual who does not produce the normal hormones, then, sexual tension of some degree will exist.

Reich asked the question, what is the outlet of sexual energy if it is neither discharged through orgasm nor released in neurotic symptoms? In his opinion, it is highly unlikely that a biological function as important as sexuality can be inhibited over an extended period of time except through the neurotic mechanism of repression. Beyond a certain limit, and beyond a period of time, intense physical work and sublimation are not, Reich believed, sufficient for expression of the sexual energy. His summary position is as follows: "Healthy individuals, that is, people capable of working and loving, direct their genitality mainly toward sexual goals . . . (Reich, 1980, p. 202)." (I will demonstrate an integration of Reich's views into a model of disruptions of the natural rhythms of sex in Chapter 3.)

Stuart and Susan Holroyd in *Sexual Loving* (1979) address the question, "Is it in any way harmful to go without sex for a long period?" Their answer is as follows. Celibacy does no harm as long as sexual energy does not get pent up with resulting feelings of frustration, but finds expression through physical and creative effort. They go on, however, to say that people who are able to so channel their sexual energy in physical and creative effort are rare. Their statement seems to be consistent with Reich's position, but put in less extreme terms. In more specific terms, the Holroyds call attention to the observation that regular sexual activity is conducive to longevity and physical vigor in later life. They also note that the sexual function will decline and the physiological processes of sex will atrophy if not used. Their conclusion is that going without sex for a long period later in life can be harmful in that it may result in a diminished level of hormones which promote physical vigor and aliveness.

In summary, I offer the following. Sexual abstinence may come about for a variety of reasons:

Possibly good reasons

(1) A side effect during illness or injury;

(2) A side effect during a period of natural grieving;

(3) A religious, ideologically based choice (e.g., not having sex outside marriage);

(4) A choice out of inconvenience (suitable partner is realistically not available);

(5) A choice for personal exploration (analogous to fasting or a period of silence or seclusion).

Not good reasons

(1) An aspect of the syndrome of depression;

(2) Neurotic fear of sexuality.

Celibacy often results from the "not good reasons," frequently with plausible "possibly good reasons" being used to cover over the core reason. If total sexual abstinence is chosen (not even masturbation), most people will build up sexual tension. The long term effects are probably deleterious, psychologically and physiologically. Celibacy is certainly contrary to sexual-aliveness. For some, there may be values which take priority over being sexually alive. For most, however, sexual-aliveness is an integral aspect of full aliveness. As Freud (Reich, 1980, p. 200) stated, " . . . sexual restriction is accompanied by a certain anxiousness and hesitation, whereas fearlessness and daring go hand in hand with sexual needs that are allowed free rein."

I think of two basic orientations to genital sex. These are the *procreation orientation* and the *pleasure orientation*. With the procreation orientation, sexuality is regarded as the means for begetting one's kind. Other considerations are secondary or absent, and success is measured in terms of conception. In contrast, the pleasure orientation is one which values the experience rather than the product of sexuality. Sex is seen, therein, as an arena for good feelings — excitement, joy, richness, fun, pleasant sensation. The contrast is between "breeding" and "playing." "Breeding sex" needs no justification in terms of its obvious necessity. "Playful sex" is of high value in its richness of both intrapersonal and interpersonal meaning.

The pleasure bond between two people is of great power and will be sought even at great cost. The importance of pleasure orientation is attested to by the extent of the technology of contraception. The whole idea in contraception, obviously, is to allow free rein of sexual pleasure unencumbered by the responsibilities which conception morally implies. A person may change sexual orientation, or even take a mixed orientation at times. The point I want to emphasize, however, is that *sexual aliveness implies full appreciation of sex for pleasure*. This is aside from the issue of casual sex versus sex in relationship. The issue is simply the correlation of aliveness and the pleasure orientation.

I began the present chapter by acknowledging the equation of being alive and being sexual, and saying that this equation deserves deeper examination. I began that examination at the level of genital sexuality. I would like, now, to expand the exploration beyond genital sexuality to that of a more broadly experienced sexuality.

In broad perspective, sex is more than a genital itch which asks to be scratched now and then. "Sexual" is a way of being-in-the-world. Ferenczi spoke of an "erotic sense of reality." What a beautiful phrase! Consider that phase for a few moments — "erotic sense of reality." This bespeaks a certain perspective, a certain way of reacting to the world. It means contacting the world passionately. *Edward L.*

Elsewhere, I have written (Smith, 1985, p. 160),

> To be sexual means to kiss the ground and embrace the trees, to roll on the grass and to smell deeply of the flowers. It means to feel excited when looking at a mountain peak and turned on when the breeze encircles the skin and tosses the hair. Such, by God and thank God, is passion.

This brings me to the nexus of sexuality and spirituality. Sexuality is sometimes experienced profoundly, thus spiritually. Spiritual meaning can emerge from the awe and the splendor of the sexual experience. Lowen (1963) has written that through sexual union an excitation can be set up which is capable of "moving the organism." In this feeling of "being moved" one can experience being part of the universal. He suggests that it is because religion can "move us," in an emotional sense, that it is a valid expression of a link with God. Sexual intercourse allows this experience of "being moved" in a direct and physical way.

The pelvis, we are told, contains mankind's deepest longings. After reaching the uncontrollable sobs of a broken heart, and screaming and kicking the stored-up rage, feeling the longing of the motherless child, perhaps then one can approach what is locked up in the pelvis. Clinical experience points the way to the depth feelings of pelvic release. *When a person is able to surrender totally to the sexual experience, when all reservation and inhibition is gone, the experience is the most transcendent possible.* When this experience has been lived, there is no need to ask again the meaning of life (Bean, 1971). This is a truth which can be spoken, but understood only by those who already know. Through sexual transcendence one can know "contact-merger-union-unity-oneness-God." Reich (1974, p. 17) proclaimed, "I do not believe that to be religious ... a man has to destroy his love life and mummify himself, body and soul ... I know that ... 'God' really exists ... God is primal cosmic energy, the love in your body, your integrity, and your perception of the nature in you and outside of you."

These ideas, shadows of the transcendent experience itself, are succinctly and boldly expressed by the poet Paul Williams (1977, pp. 45–46) when he writes, "Fucking is wholly spiritual. It is also physical. ... *Making* love is physical, and spiritual." He has developed this theme in a volume of verse titled *Coming*. On the back cover he concludes, "Coming is the same as being. It's what we're here for — there's nothing else to do."

Sexual union can be seen as fundamentally a religious act, a coming together of female and male energies. This was the case in many early civilizations. Examples include Ishtar in Babylonia, Isis in Egypt, Aphrodite in Greece, and Diana in Rome. The mystery religions of both the East and the West have taken this view on sex, namely, *experience in the flesh leads to the divine* (Mann, 1973). Interestingly, this doctrine is not developed in mainstream Judeo-Christian thought. There is, however, ample evidence of sexual phrasing in the writings of the early Christian mystics. And certainly the "Song of Songs" in the Bible's midst has been of embarrassment to both Christians and Jews (Adam, 1976).

India is certainly a country that has most openly expressed the divinity of sexuality. Her religious art is replete with overt sexual themes. For a very readable discourse, lavishly illustrated, on India's erotic religious art I recommend Adam's (1976) *Wandering in Eden*.

The best-known religiously based system in which sexual practice is explicity elevated to religious ritual is Tantric Buddhism. In this Yogic system it is said "Buddhahood resides in the vulva of woman (Adam, 1976, p. 29)." Correspondingly, the "lingam" (phallus), too, is worshiped. In the practice of Tantra there are elaborate procedures aimed at intensification of the senses and the recognition of the sacredness of the sexual acts performed.

Perhaps Nietzsche (Apophthegms and Interludes, 75) summarized it when he wrote, "The degree and nature of a man's sensuality extends to the highest attitudes of his spirit."

With orgasm there can be an obliteration of ego and thus identification with cosmic processes. It is as if the ego dies, as called attention to by the French who refer to orgasm as "la petite mort," or "the little death." The usual experience which follows the ego obliteration is that of rebirth. So sex may provide a microcosm for dying and being reborn. With the rebirth comes renewal and rejuvenation. What can be more spiritual than this?

Alan Watts (Adam, 1976) proclaimed that no matter how many philosophies one studies, how many spiritual exercises one practices, how many scriptures one searches, and how many spiritual teachers one consults, in the end one returns to the surprising fact of eating, sleeping, feeling, breathing, moving about, the surprising fact of being alive. This, he said, surprising fact of being alive is the "supreme experience of religion." And is aliveness ever more profoundly felt than in the sexual embrace?

2. The Natural Rhythms of Sex

There is a natural rhythm to sex. That rhythm is characterized by contacting and withdrawing. When the sexual urge arises there is movement toward making appropriate contact with a suitable sexual object, and then, following satisfaction, there is a withdrawal from that object. The cycle is one of contact-satisfaction-withdrawal, based on the socially edited biological urge for sex.

I want to offer a model for the description and understanding of this psychobiological unit of living, the Sexual Contact/Withdrawal Cycle. This model, specific to sexuality in the present writing, derives from a more general application of the Contact/Withdrawal Cycle to various human needs (Smith, 1979, 1985, 1986).

The wanting of sex involves both a need and an array of preferences. The need is basic and biological, whereas the preferences are what lend a certain flavor or style to one's sexuality. Preferences tend to be negotiable and sometimes to evolve and change over time. It is preferences which are the individualistic

23

expression of the more universal need for sex. Just as there are individual differences in the strength of the basic psychobiological need for sex, there are enormous individual differences in what is sexually preferred and in the strengths of those preferences.

Insofar as preferences are the specific choices one makes when there are options for meeting the sexual need, the sexual urge is the "what" or content of sexual aliveness and the preferences are expressed in the "how" or style of sexual aliveness. An important application of this need-preference distinction is in understanding some aspects of sexual incompatibility. If two people are vastly different in their sexual need, then a sexually exclusive relationship may be very difficult. This follows from the relative nonnegotiability of the need. (I am not considering here pathological conditions of absence of desire, but rather the normal range of sexual need.) If, however, an incompatibility is with respect to preferred style of sexual expression, that is potentially negotiable.

Returning to the *Sexual Contact/Withdrawal Cycle (SCWC)*, there are several steps which can be described between the arising of the Want (need or preference) and the satisfaction of that Want. When the Want arises, a state of physiological Arousal follows. This Arousal is a state of organismic tension and excitement, a mobilization to a state of higher energy. Although in evidence throughout the organism, this "turn on" is most obvious in the engorged genitals and female lubrication.

This heightened energy state which results from Arousal is differentiated and subjectively experienced as sexual Emotions — love and lust. By love I mean the feelings of tenderness, caring, affection for the other. Lust, on the other hand, is the desire for sexual pleasure, the selfish wish for orgastic satisfaction. The particular Emotion felt will be a blend of love and lust, each contributing its component of strength. Psychobiologically, the Emotion is the subjective experience of the energy flow in the body.

Sexual Emotion, as the word E-*motion* implies, calls forth Action, or the movement of energy into the musculoskeletal system. Action is concrete bodily involvement.

Action leads naturally to Interaction, the contacting of another. Interaction occurs at what in Gestalt therapy is termed the "contact boundary." So, the participants share in the various forms of sexual contact.

If all has gone well, the final stage of the Contact Episode is reached — Satisfaction. So, the Contact Episode consists of the stages of Want (need and preferences) → Arousal → Emotion (love and lust) → Action → Interaction → Satisfaction. Once sexual Satisfaction is experienced there is a natural Withdrawal, until the sexual urge arises once more as the Want. The SCWC includes, then, a Contact Episode and a Withdrawal Episode, with the former being much more complex.

The first half of the Contact Episode (Want → Arousal → Emotion) is importantly related to Awareness. In the case of natural sexual functioning the person is aware of wanting sex (Need), wanting a particular form of sex (Preference), feeling excited and energized (Arousal), and feeling a blend of love and lust (Emotion). It is this Awareness, this knowing of one's present state which focuses one for the second or Expression half of the Contact Episode (Action → Interaction → Satisfaction). Awareness means being tuned in to one's self, being in touch with the internal streamings of life energy. So, Awareness is the guide to Expression.

Some people are more attuned to Awareness to the relative neglect of Expression, while others find Expression to be easy, but lack in clear Awareness. These two orientations define the poles of the obsessive-impulsive dimension. Obsessive people may know acutely their desire for sexual contact, feel their excitement and ache with their loving, lusting feelings, but find expression of their sexuality difficult and frightening. These are the people who suffer with chronic sexual tension. The opposite situation is with the impulsive person who moves easily into sexual expression but without benefit of the focus given by Awareness. Awareness includes the consideration of appropriateness both in terms of timing and choice of sexual partner. Without that the impulsive person inevitably gets into trouble with others over her or his sexual expression. I'm getting away from the focus of the present chapter here and anticipating the next chapter in which I will talk about disruptions of the natural rhythms of sex. In order to understand those disruptions and thereby be in a position to reestablish the natural rhythm, I believe a careful and thorough understanding of the SCWC is important. So, let's return to the model.

Satisfaction through sexual contact requires both Awareness and Expression. If either of those two aspects of contact is deficient, sexual aliveness will be diminished. The steps in the SCWC are cumulative, each one depending for its success on the full and effective development of all previous steps. If any step is not allowed to develop in its fullness all of the proceeding steps will be less well formed and the ultimate Satisfaction will be diminished or missed completely.

The SCWC model is complicated by the presence of feedback loops such that a later step in the cycle may clarify and enhance an earlier step. For example, a person who is sexually aroused may approach the object of her or his love, and upon touching the lover the sexual arousal is magnified greatly. In this example the step of Interaction is fed back to an earlier stage in the cycle, the stage of Arousal → Emotion. It is as if there are reverberating waves in the SCWC which enhance the previous steps as each new step is taken. Clearly, then, sexual awareness is often increased by sexual expression. So, Awareness focuses and guides Expression, while Expression clarifies Awareness. When I touch my lover, I may know more clearly my sexual want, feel my excitement soar, and be more filled with love and lust. And so it is that any step in the SCWC may reverberate within any of the previous steps.

Before moving on I want to note that these feedback loops can serve to correct as well as to enhance previous steps in the SCWC. If my Action → Interaction sequence is not congruent with my Awareness, the feedback will allow my Awareness to change, and in turn, then redirect my Expression. Let's imagine, for instance, that I am angry with my lover and she approaches me sexually. For various reasons I may not be aware of my anger and so, in my unawareness, I proceed into sexual contact. My sexual Arousal → Emotion probably will lack in fullness and energy, but I move on to Action → Interaction anyway. As I touch her and she touches me, I become aware, I sense the discrepancy between what I am doing and what I am now feeling. Perhaps I lose my erection. The message to me is that I have another Want, the need to process my anger with my lover, which is taking preeminence over my sexual Want. In this case, the feedback from my Action → Interaction informed me that my appropriate stage in my SCWC was that of Withdrawal. (As I mentioned in an opening paragraph of this chapter, the SCWC is a special case of the general Contact/Withdrawal Cycle model which applies to all human

Wants. In the above example my pre-eminent Want was to process anger. Upon satisfaction of that want, I would move into
Withdrawal and that cycle would be complete. Than I would be
ready for the next emergent want, perhaps that would be sex, and
a SCWC would begin, free from the "unfinished business" of my
anger.)

I have found the SCWC model to be extremely helpful for
describing and understanding sexual behavior. Once this model is
thoroughly understood, sexual problems can be identified easily
and understood as interruptions in the natural Contact/
Withdrawal flow. But, more about that in succeeding chapters.
At this point I want to elaborate upon the basic model. (See
Figure 1.)

In *Love and Orgasm* Alexander Lowen (1965) distinguished
sensuality from sexuality. He elaborates upon the sensualist as one
who is primarily interested in those aspects of sex which involve
stimulation and excitement and the sexualist as one who aims for
the pleasure release or orgasm. This is an interesting distinction to
draw as it relates to the SCWC. The Awareness half of the Contact
Episode may be thought of as relating to sensuality. For during the
Want → Arousal → Emotion sequence the focus is on raising the level
of awareness of the sexual need and the specific preference as to the
style of sexual behavior wanted, the organismic excitement, and
the feelings of love and lust. The pleasure here is a pleasure of
sensing and feeling.

In the Action → Interaction → Satisfaction sequence the focus
shifts to the pleasure of the end goal, the orgastic release. So, the
Expression half of the Contact Episode corresponds to the activity
of what Lowen identifies as the sexualist. As is clear from the
previous discussion of the SCWC, both the Awareness and the
Expression functions must be well developed in order that Satisfaction can be experienced. Or, stated in terms of sensuality and sexuality, sexual satisfaction requires both sensuality and sexuality (in
the narrow sense of that word). And, following the above mentioned
tendency of some people to be more attuned to Awareness (the
obsessives) and others to be more attuned to Expression (the
impulsives) we find the equivalent to Lowen's sensualist and
sexualist distinction.

The Contact/Withdrawal rhythm is one of expansion and

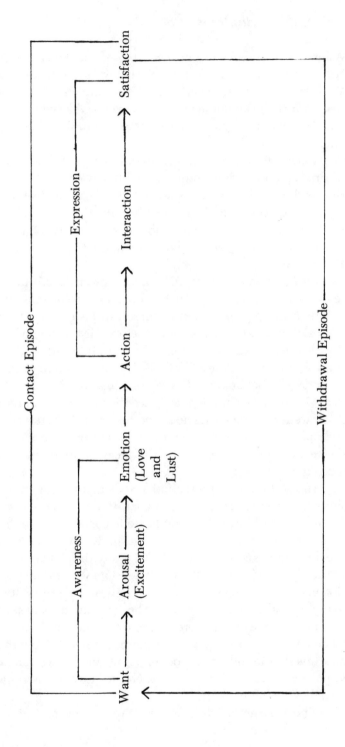

Figure 1. Sexual Contact/Withdrawal Cycle (SCWC)

contraction. The Contact Episode involves a movement out into the world for sexual contact with the expectation of sexual Satisfaction. The person chosen for the sexual contact is given a positive valence and is moved toward. Upon Satisfaction the chosen person is given a neutral valence (with respect to the sexual Want), and one withdraws in indifference. This Withdrawal is a relaxed contraction away from the source of satisfaction. Thus, the rhythm of Contact and Withdrawal is one of expansion and contraction.

What I have just said relates to a central point in the theories of Wilhelm Reich (1973). Reich identified what he saw as a primary antithesis of organismic life, that being Pleasure (expansion) and Anxiety (contraction). Expansion and contraction are distinguished by the direction of energy flow; "you reach out with your life energy when you feel well and loving, and . . . you retract it to the center of your body when you are afraid" (Reich, quoted in Mann and Hoffman, 1980, p. 91). What Reich is describing here corresponds to the expansive, pleasurable movement, both internal to the organism and of the organism in the world, of the Contact Episode of the SCWC.

Reich did not, however, distinguish between the *relaxed contraction* which follows satisfaction and the *anxious contraction* which is fear. I think it is more accurate to distinguish three poles: Expansion (Contact Episode, pleasure), Relaxed Contraction (Withdrawal Episode, quiet), and Anxious Contraction (Interrupted Contact Episode or Avoidance, anxiety). The third pole, pertaining to Avoidance or the interruption of the Contact Episode, is the focus of the following chapter.

Reich (1973, p. 88) in referring to the psychobiological level, has written that "all biological impulses and organ sensations can be reduced to *expansion* (elongation, dilation) and *contraction* (shrinking, constriction)." These he relates to the autonomic nervous system as follows: "the parasympathetic (vagus) always functions where there is expansion, dilation, hyperemia, turgor, and pleasure. Conversely, the *sympathetic* nerves function whenever the organism contracts, blood is withdrawn from the periphery and pallor, anxiety, and pain appear." Although oversimplified, Reich's account is consistent with recent views of the functioning of the autonomic nervous system and the psychophysiological basis of psychosomatic disorders (for a

Figure 2. Characteristics of the Contact Episode and the Withdrawal Episode of the Sexual Contact/Withdrawal Cycle

Contact Episode	*Withdrawal Episode*
Organismic expansion	Relaxed contraction
Pleasure	Quiet
Partner given + valence	Partner given 0 valence
Organismic elongation	Organismic shortening
Organismic dilation	Organismic relaxation
"Yes"	Disinterested "No"
Movement toward partner	Withdrawal into self
Muscular action	Muscles in relaxed tonus
Peripheral excitation	
Central discharge	
PANS dominant	
Anabolism dominant	

discussion of the psychophysiology of psychosomatic disorders I recommend Gannon, 1981).

Louis Saeger (1980) has also discussed the basic physiological activities involved in movement toward the world and withdrawal from the world. Simply stated, stimuli, either actual or imagined (symbolic) are processed through central integrating mechanisms of the central nervous system, involving the limbic system and the hypothalamic centers. These central integrating mechanisms send impulses to the autonomic nervous system (ANS) which leads to an integrated response involving every system of the body. One system affected is the endocrine system, which then releases hormones to either stimulate or inhibit the energetic functions of specific tissues and organs and to potentiate direct effects of sympathetic (SANS) or parasympathetic (PANS) innervation. The endocrine effect is basically either to mobilize or to conserve energy. And, at the level of the tissues and organs, the endocrine response and the effects of the parasympathetic (PANS) and sympathetic (SANS) portions of the autonomic nervous system (ANS) combine to create a specific metabolic and energetic activity profile for the emotion in question. And, finally, the emotional energy is mobilized through the musculo-skeletal system.

Such, in very brief and simplified form, is the psychophysiology of the SCWC. (I will elaborate later when discussing some specific problems in sexuality.)

In a sense, organismic expansion is a psychobiological statement of "yes," whereas organismic contraction is a statement of "no." It is this "yes" and "no" which are the bases of the expansion of Contact and the relaxed contraction of Withdrawal. Herein, in this "yes" and "no" is the regulation of the natural rhythm of sex.

3. Disruptions of the Natural Rhythms of Sex

As long as the *Sexual Contact/Withdrawal Cycles* proceed smoothly, with a rhythm of sexual needs arising and being satisfied, there is a natural and healthy psychological state. The problem is when this natural rhythm is disrupted. In terms of the psychological functioning of a person, the problem for that person is the self-interruption of the natural sexual rhythm. This leads me to a definition of sexual psychopathology. I define *sexual psychopathology as any pattern of habitual self-interruption in the Sexual Contact/Withdrawal Cycle.* (This is the specifically sexual case of a more general definition of psychopathology I have offered — Smith, 1979, 1985.) Such habitual self-interruptions take priority over natural sexual expression, which is rooted in the "wisdom of the organism." This overriding of that subtle inner voice which guides natural, organismically-based living leads to a cumulative sexual self-alienation.

In looking at the SCWC it is clear that there are several points

33

at which partial or complete self-interruption can occur. The locus of self-interruption in the cycle is a major factor in the variety of specific forms which sexual problems can assume. Let us look in detail at the points of self-interruption.

First is the choice of being aware of what one wants. This includes both awareness of the sexual need and the awareness of one's preference in terms of the style in which that need is to be satisfied. To be unaware of what one wants, sexually, is to stay in the Withdrawal phase of the SCWC. This is not to say that one could not be a participant in someone else's SCWC, but it means that the person not aware of her or his want is not living out a self-initiated experience based on the wisdom of the inner urge. A frequent symptom of a self-interruption at this point in the SCWC is boredom. If there is a sexual need developing, but this is not allowed into awareness, the person will probably experience boredom — "I want something, but I don't know what. Nothing seems to be the right thing."

Another aspect of the awareness problem at the point of the Want is the lack of differentiation between the sexual Need and the sexual Preference. This can manifest in either of two ways. First, and more commonly, the preferred style of sexuality is mistaken for a Need, so that nothing else will do. When the Preference is regarded as a Need, there is a reaction to its being denied far out of proportion to the mere inconvenience of that denial. This confusion of awareness lends a rigid quality to sexuality, with a lack of variety and experimentation. An example of this is the patient who says, "I can only have an orgasm if I'm on top, and I don't even want to try that other stuff." Second, but less commonly, the sexual Need may be regarded as only a Preference. In this situation the person may disregard the sexual Need for extended periods of time. Such a patient may report forgetting to have sex, or being too busy to get around to it. In either case the loss of awareness of the sexual Want (Need and Preference differentiated) precludes the smooth flow of sexual cycles.

The second point for self-interruption of the SCWC is the junction between the Want and Arousal. This means an interruption before sexual excitement is allowed to develop. A person who is interrupting the cycle here may be aware of wanting sex, but does not feel aroused. It is as if her or his body is unwilling to proceed.

In a man, this is evidenced by a lack of penile erection and in a woman, by lack of genital engorgement and lubrication.

The transition from Arousal to Emotion is the third site for self-interruption. In this case the person is not organismically differentiating her or his excitement into the feelings of love and lust. Instead, he or she will only be agitated, nervous, or tense.

Of special interest and importance is the fourth point of self-interruption, the transition from Emotion to Action, for this is the transition from Awareness to that of Expression. To block at this point one is stopping the flow of energy into the musculoskeletal system for processing. Whereas the Want → Arousal → Emotion sequence belongs to the realm of the autonomic nervous system, the movement into Action → Interaction involves the voluntary nervous system whereby skeletal muscles are activated. This decision to remain in the realm of preexpression is especially common in the oversocialized, those patients who ruminate and obsess for fear of "misbehaving" sexually.

If the transition into the realm of Expression is made, the next decision is whether or not to allow the Action to become interactive. This is the fifth point for self-interruption, the transition to Interaction with someone who would allow for the potential Satisfaction of the sexual urge. This block may appear either by the person not interacting at all, or by her or his choosing a partner who is unwilling to provide the appropriate Interaction.

Even though all of the previous steps have been taken, it is possible to self-interrupt between Interaction and Satisfaction. The person who blocks here at the sixth point of self-interruption does not allow herself or himself that final step and goal of sexual contact. In this case, then, we see a person who is sexually active and yet unsatisfied. This is an issue once more of awareness.

The seventh decision point, whether to flow or self-interrupt, follows Satisfaction. The organismically natural step is to withdraw when Satisfaction is complete. But the Contact Episode may be prolonged beyond the point of Satisfaction, thus interrupting the flow into Withdrawal. When this is done, the prolonged Contact becomes forced, unnatural, and what was satisfying becomes noxious and disgusting. This is the person who hangs on and on, ruining what could have been a good sexual encounter.

In summary, one can choose to interrupt the SCWC at any of

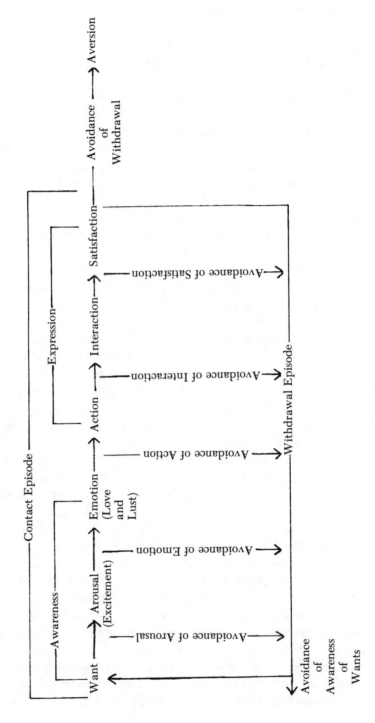

Figure 3. Sexual Contact/Withdrawal Cycle with Avoidances

seven junctures. Such a self-interruption is a short-circuiting of the ongoing flow of the psychobiological process of sexual life. The issue is, do I allow a natural sexual aliveness, or do I override the sexual rhythm revealed through the wisdom of my organism and interrupt my flow? The decision to self-interrupt results in leaving a Want unmet, and thus the accumulation of "unfinished business." Each self-interruption is an Avoidance. What is avoided is the next step in the SCWC, and ultimately an avoidance of the experience of sexual aliveness.

So far in this chapter I have been discussing the forms which disruptions of the natural rhythm of sex can take. Now that the *what* of sexual psychopathology has been covered, two questions logically arise: The first is *why* would one want to interrupt the SCWC, thus disrupting a natural rhythm of sexual aliveness? The second question is, given that one wants to interrupt one's SCWCs, *how* can one do so?

First, I will address the question of "why" one would interrupt one's natural rhythm of sexual aliveness. The key to understanding these self-interruptions is to understand the dynamics of the "toxic introject." What has happened to most of us is that we received messages from parents or parenting figures which discouraged or prohibited our sexuality. During early development the treatment of the child by parents, grandparents, and other parenting figures encourages and supports natural aliveness or discourages and forbids it. If the child is punished, by scoldings, shaming, or physical punishment, for showing natural curiosity about her or his body, or others' bodies, a message of prohibition is likely to be internalized.

So, a parent's telling the child "Don't touch yourself there" when the child is found fondling her or his genitals becomes the basis for interrupting a natural process. Now imagine how indelibly etched the message could be if it is said firmly, or shouted, or paired with a threat of punishment, or even paired with a slap or worse.

So it is that during the early years we may have been given messages that were not in support of our aliveness (biopositive messages) but were messages demanding diminished aliveness or even deadness (bionegative messages). These messages may have been given verbally or nonverbally.

Primarily because of the profound dependence of the child on the parenting figures for its very survival, the bionegative message may be "swallowed whole," that is, introjected. Secondarily, this process of introjection is facilitated by the fact that the child has very little life experience against which to judge the bionegative messages. Since these bionegative messages are poisonous to healthy sexual development and natural sexual living, they can be termed "toxic introjects." As the child grows older, and its sphere of living expands to include teachers, clergy, parents of friends, sitters, and so on, these people can also be sources for further toxic introjects. As adolescence is approached, there is frequently an increase in the intensity of toxic introjects given to the person regarding her or his emerging sexuality.

There are two components to the toxic introject. The first is the content, or specific prohibition. The content is often in the form of a "should" or a "should not." Frequently the toxic introject is heard by patients as voices in their heads. It is as if someone speaks up and says "You should . . . " or "You should not . . . " or some synonym of that. The second component of the toxic introject is the "catastrophic expectation," or the threat that if the toxic introject is disobeyed, something awful will happen. Since most of these toxic messages are introjected during the early years, the catastrophic expectation is very often that the person will lose love.

Let us take a simple example of the dynamics of a toxic introject. A child may have been scolded for "playing doctor" with a friend when very young. The look of disapproval and the harsh words of "Don't do that. That's dirty! That's naughty!" may have left the toxic introject which consists of exactly those words, or a summary version such as "You shouldn't be sexual." Sometimes the patient does not recall the words until some considerable therapy work has been done, but nevertheless reacts *as if* those words were being spoken. The threat may have been spoken explicitly, or it may have been implied, *as if* the grown-up said "And if you do that dirty, naughty thing, I won't love you any more." This toxic introject may give the child a set about sexuality so that further messages and information which are consistent with that set are introjected to reinforce the original toxic introject.

I term these "primary toxic introjects" (early toxic introjects, usually received during the first five years or so) and "secondary toxic introjects" (later toxic introjects, received sometime after the first five years or so, and reinforcing of the primary toxic introjects), respectively. Just as the primary toxic introject has both a content and a catastrophic expectation, the secondary toxic introjects have both components as well. But, since secondary toxic introjects are received at a later age, they tend both in content and catastrophic expectation to *appear* more reasonable. In our example, the person may be told around early adolescence that sex is dangerous. Perhaps a parent or teacher says "Don't have sex. You'll get a venereal disease." This secondary toxic introject reinforces what the person already believed.

The primary and secondary toxic introjects jointly determine the person's "sexual script," or the sexual belief system and rules which will be acted out until such time that it is examined and different decisions are made. In our example, the sexual script is a toxic one, being based on bionegative messages rather than biopositive ones. A toxic sexual script is usually maintained, unexamined and unchallenged, throughout one's life. The result is a longstanding conflict between the natural urge for sexual aliveness and the toxic sexual script made up from toxic introjects calling for deadness. Once the toxic messages have been introjected, the threat of the catastrophic expectations leaves the person phobic with regard to sexual aliveness. To continue our example, the person is scripted to be sexually deadened. The primary toxic introject stated that sex is dirty and naughty, with the catastrophic expectation being that if he or she does that dirty and naughty thing he or she won't be loved by the parents. The secondary toxic introject in our example stated that our person should not have sex, and the catastrophic expectation is that if he or she has sex he or she will get a disease. Thus, our person has a toxic sexual script: Do not have sex, for it is dirty; if you do it you must feel unloved, and you will get a disease.

The greater the number and/or severity of the toxic introjects concerning sexuality, the more sexually phobic the person is, and the less sexual aliveness the person allows. The essence of limiting sexual aliveness is the self-interruption of the SCWC. The point of self-interruption in the SCWC which is chosen is determined by the sexual script or more precisely, the content of the toxic introjects.

To finish our example, the toxic introjects mentioned, both

primary and secondary, said "You should not have sex." In both the primary and secondary toxic introjects the implication was not to be interactive with sex. We can predict that in the case of just these toxic introjects, not modified or complicated by other toxic introject content, our person would self-interrupt her or his sexual flow at the junction between Action and Interaction. In clinical practice I have found that the toxic introjects operate with the dynamic described here.

The reason for self-interruptions in the SCWC is thus explained in terms of the dynamics of the sexual toxic introjects, or as they are jointly experienced, the toxic sexual script. A person will flow in her or his SCWC to the point at which a toxic introject intrudes with its prohibition and threat. At that point the person deadens and interferes with the natural sexual rhythm.

Having described "why" one would choose to self-interrupt the SCWC, I now turn to the question of "how." The self-interruption is an avoidance of the next step in the SCWC, as I showed in the discussion above. An avoidance is accomplished by means of four pathological mechanisms, those mechanisms often working in combination and in synergy. Satisfying contact, as I have shown, involves Arousal, focusing of one's aroused energy through Awareness, and enactment of that energy (Action → Interaction). The four pathological mechanisms focus on the quieting of Arousal, the clouding of Awareness, the nonenactment of Action, and the nonenactment of Interaction, respectively.

The result of the use of these mechanisms of Avoidance can be either a complete self-interruption of the flow of the SCWC, or just a diminishing of that flow. The former means a complete avoidance of the experience beyond the point of self-interruption, whereas the latter means a diminished or weakened experience beyond the point of self-interruption. I want to borrow the terminology used by Erv and Miriam Polster (1973) to distinguish the stopping of an impulse — Block, and the diminished expression of an impulse — Inhibition. So, a self-interruption in a SCWC may be a Block or may be an Inhibition.

When there is an Inhibition there is some degree of energy flow into the next steps of the SCWC, and therefore the possibility of multiple sites of avoidance, either multiple Inhibitions or Inhibition followed by a Block. As an example, a person who has a Block at the juncture between Emotion and Action does not behave sexually and therefore doesn't have a problem with the realm of Action → Interaction → Satisfaction. This person's sexual script may be "It's O.K. to feel sexual, but don't act on those feelings." A second person may self-interrupt at the same juncture (Emotion → Action), but with an Inhibition rather than a Block. Her or his script may be "It's O.K. to feel sexual, but it's better not to act on those feelings. If you do act on them, be sure not to enjoy yourself." In this case we could predict an Inhibition of Action and a Block to Satisfaction.

I want to save the detailed discussion of the four pathological mechanisms for self-interrupting the natural sexual rhythm (quieting Arousal, clouding Awareness, nonenactment of Action, and nonenactment of Interaction) for chapters four, five, six and seven, respectively.

Just as the natural sexual Contact Episode involves aggressive Expansion into the world and natural sexual Withdrawal involves Relaxed Contraction into the self, the self-interruption of the SCWC is an Anxious Contraction away from the world, an Avoidance of sexual aliveness. And thus, anxiety can be seen as the signal that a self-interruption in the natural sexual rhythm is taking place. Anxiety means avoidance of the next step in the flow of the SCWC, and is in response to the catastrophic expectation threatened by the toxic introject. To relate this to what Reich (1973, p. 288) has written, " . . . all biological impulses and organ sensations can be reduced to *expansion* (elongation, dilation) and *contraction* (shrinking, constriction)." In relating these functions to the autonomic nervous system (ANS) Reich (1973, p. 288) stated " . . . the parasympathetic (vagus) always functions where there is expansion, dilation, hyperemia, turgor, and pleasure. Conversely, the *sympathetic* nerves function whenever the organism contracts, blood is withdrawn from the periphery and pallor, anxiety and pain appear."

In elaborating the sympathetic nervous system response, Saeger (1980, p. 42) has stated: "The blood is literally withdrawn 'away from the world' in SANS response: there is peripheral vasoconstriction with concomitant stimulation of the heart (in extreme cases, palpitation and tachycardia). . . . The opposite occurs in PANS activation." Following further discussion of ANS profiles, Saeger concluded that the ANS profile determines the

Figure 4. Characteristics of the Contact Episode,
the Withdrawal Episode, and Avoidance in the
Sexual Contact/Withdrawal Cycle

Contact Episode	*Withdrawal Episode*	*Avoidance*
Organismic expansion	Relaxed contraction	Anxious contraction
Pleasure	Quiet	Anxiety
Partner given + valence	Partner given 0 valence	Partner given − valence
Organismic elongation	Organismic shortening	Organismic shrinking
Organismic dilation	Organismic relaxation	Organismic constriction
"Yes"	Disinterested "No"	Anxious "No"
Movement toward partner	Withdrawal into self	Movement away from partner
Muscular action	Muscles in relaxed tonus	Muscular tension
Peripheral excitation		Peripheral discharge
Central discharge		Central excitation
PANS dominant		SANS dominant
Anabolism dominant		Catabolism dominant

direction of flux of body liquids of the whole organism, and that SANS hyperactivation describes the anxiety response. Pleasure is described by PANS activity or flux of fluids toward the world.

Under normal circumstances the PANS and SANS activity are in balance with the activity of one or the other becoming temporarily dominant according to the needs of the organism. There may, however, be a decided shift towards a chronic PANS or SANS dominance, resulting in an imbalance and in turn a functional disorder. The imbalances are termed "parasympathicotonia" and "sympathicotonia," respectively. As Steen and Montagu (1959, p. 124) state, "The influence of emotional states on this delicate balance of the autonomic nervous system is a matter of common observation."

The very recent thinking in the area of psychophysiology is consistent with the preceding. Gannon (1981, p. 21) offers this summary, for instance: " . . . an individual's personality, experience, and socialization, that is, one's learning history, may instill a set to view specific stimuli as threatening or stressful. In such a case, any variables which influence the self-reported intensity of stress may affect the degree, direction, and patterning of autonomic activity."

And in terms of sexuality, specifically, Heimen and Hatch (1981, p. 226) report that " . . . it is generally agreed that the vast majority of sexual dysfunctions are primarily of psychological etiology. . . . [T]he primary symptomatology of sexual dysfunction is indeed physiological, even when etiology is psychological."

Kaplan (1974) in *The New Sex Therapy* has taken the position that anxiety is behind all sexual dysfunction, in that anxiety interferes psychologically and physiologically with the sexual response. This position is a reminder of the work of Wolpe (1958) in which he presented his hypothesis of "reciprocal inhibition." This hypothesis states that the anxiety response and sexual arousal are mutually inhibiting processes with neurophysiological basis. The model which I am offering, the SCWC, is consistent with these views, but involves a great deal of refinement and elaboration of detail.

At this point we can complete Figure 2 (of the previous chapter), which contained a summary of the characteristics of the Contact Episode and the Withdrawal Episode of the Sexual Contact/Withdrawal Cycle. To that material are added the characteristics of Avoidance: see Figure 4.

4. Sexual Deadening Through Lowered Arousal

In this chapter I want to explore in some detail the dynamics of the first of the four pathological mechanisms by which one can self-interrupt the SCWC. This is the mechanism of inhibiting or blocking Arousal. Since this mechanism is "upstream" from the mechanisms which interfere with the Expression portion of the Contact Episode, it is clinically found always to accompany the nonenactment of the Action → Interaction sequence. In addition, this mechanism works extremely well in synergy with the clouding of Awareness. So, in a way the inhibition of Arousal is a keystone to the whole structure of the interrupted cycle of sexual contact and withdrawal. It is the sexual arousal which is the driving force for sexual contact. Without excitement there is no sex.

The quelling of sexual excitement can be seen through metaphor as the turning off of the valve which controls the sexual flow. It is that the amount of sexual energy which is made available for sexual feelings and expression is regulated at the point of

Arousal. The greater the inhibition of this excitement, the less sexual the person will feel and the less sexuality will be expressed.

Even though the quelling of excitement is focused at the juncture in the SCWC between Want and Arousal, it can serve a secondary role in self-interruptions at other junctures, as I have explained. But, for now, I want to stay with the primary focus of this mechanism. Given that this is *where* a person is self-interrupting, *what* is the problem experienced, *why* is the self-interruption at this point in the SCWC and *how* does the person accomplish the inhibition or block?

What sexual problem is identified or experienced? The person who is inhibited or blocked between Want and Arousal is likely to identify as a problem a lack of excitement. Even though this person reports that he or she wants sex, there is a lack of getting "turned on." Bodily arousal is subdued. If this person goes through with sex, it will be without heavy breathing, perspiring, fast heart beat, and such indications of physiological arousal. There will be low energy sex at best. So, this person may complain of being tired or of not having much energy for being sexual. More dramatically the man may fail to get an erection or lose his erection and the woman may not lubricate.

Why self-interrupt at this particular juncture? Primary blocking or inhibiting at this point is called for when the message of the toxic introject is "You should stay calm" or stated in the negative form, "You should not get sexually excited." With such a message there is no room for getting "turned on" without threat of the implied catastrophe (the "catastrophic expectation" which is a component of the toxic introject). I have heard people who have this toxic introject say things which identify hard breathing as vulgar and perspiring as morally bad. I recall one such woman saying with strong feeling, "Oh, I just hate to perspire!" So a statement to the effect that breathing hard or perspiring is "not nice" may be evidence of a toxic introject which prohibits excitement. For a man the message may be, "It's a sin to get a 'hard on'."

This leaves the question of the how of self-interruption of Arousal. *The basic method for quelling excitement is the reduction of air by means of improper breathing.* This is so important to understand that I want to delve deeply into the mechanics of breathing.

Normal breathing is an involuntary rhythmic activity under the control of the autonomic nervous system. Fourteen to eighteen breaths are taken per minute, on the average, or twenty to twenty-five thousand breaths per day. With this many breaths there is a considerable cumulative effect when the normal breathing is altered. One of the interesting aspects of breathing is that the autonomic control can be overridden by conscious voluntary control. In this way both the depth and rate of breathing can be made greater or less. In normal breathing there is a smooth, rhythmic action which involves the entire body. Inspiration consists of an outward movement of the abdomen as the abdominal muscles relax and the diaphragm contracts. With this the chest expands. The pelvis rocks slightly so that the sacrum moves back. At the same time the neck arches back slightly. On inspiration there is a slight arching back of the entire torso reducing the distance between the cranial and sacral ends. This wave of inspiration can be felt from the head to the genitals and even down to the feet, when it is deep. After a brief pause the wave reverses. So, in expiration, as the diaphragm relaxes the abdomen moves back in place from its protruded position and the chest relaxes from its expansion. The pelvis rocks forward as the head returns to normal position with the arch taken out of the neck. On expiration the cranial-sacral distance is increased. Here, too, is a brief pause as the breathing cycle is completed.

What I have described is *abdominal or diaphragmatic breathing.* On a slightly more technical level this is how diaphragmatic breathing takes place. When the diaphragm contracts there is an increase in the vertical diameter of the thoracic cavity and thereby a reduction in intrathoracic pressure. Since the outside pressure is then greater, the result is an inflow of air through the nose or mouth. On the exhalation the diaphragm relaxes while the recoil of the stretched costal cartilages and stretched lungs, and the weight of the thoracic wall increases the intrathoracic pressure. This forces the air out through the nose or mouth. In normal, quiet respiration, then, the inhalation is active (the diaphragm contracts) and the exhalation is passive (the diaphragm relaxes).

During strenuous muscular exertion or voluntary heavy breathing there is a different pattern. This is forced respiration known as *costal or thoracic breathing.* In thoracic breathing the external intercostal muscles and several synergic muscles actually force an expansion of the rib cage, thus bringing about the reduction of intrathoracic pressure. In forced breathing the exhalation is also active. The abdominal muscles, internal intercostal muscles, serratus posterior inferior, and quadratus lumborum all contract, thus reducing the size of the thoracic cavity and squeezing the air out (Steen and Montagu, 1959).

These patterns described are the natural patterns of breathing—abdominal breathing for times of nonexertion and thoracic breathing to meet the need for more rapid turnover of air at times of exertion.

What is focal to our purpose here is how full sexual excitement is avoided by means of unnatural breathing patterns. More generally, Lowen (1965) has stated that every emotional problem is reflected in a disturbance of breathing. And, of course in the SCWC Emotion is one step "downstream" from Arousal. Perls (1969) as early as the late 1940s wrote about the connection of breathing with various psychological states, noting that shallow breathing and sighing are connected with depression, chronic yawning with boredom, and fighting for breath with anxiety. In another work a few years later Perls (Perls, Hefferline, and Goodman, 1951) stated clearly and emphatically that anxiety is the experience of breathing difficulty during blocked excitement. So anxiety is experienced when more air is needed to support a growing excitement and breathing is restricted such that the needed air is not provided. When the lungs are relatively immobilized by muscular constriction of the chest, the air to support excitement is denied. The healthy response to a growing sexual excitement is to breathe more deeply. If, however, sexual Arousal is forbidden by one's toxic introjects and the sexual script calls for shutting down the SCWC before full Arousal is experienced, tensing of the muscles of the breathing apparatus can be effective. With this pattern there may be feelings of anxiety and irritability.

There are two typical disturbances of breathing which have been identified by Lowen (1965). The first is a pattern in which respiration is with the chest, the abdomen being excluded for the most part. The abdominal muscles are held in contraction and the diaphragm immobilized. The chest itself is held in a deflated position and so is narrowed and constricted. I suggest that you, the reader, breathe in this manner for a minute or so. Explore for yourself the feeling state which accompanies the lowered oxygen uptake of this breathing pattern.

The second pattern of disturbed breathing involves diaphragmatic action, but with the chest immobilized in the expanded position. With the chest held in the expanded position the lungs do not empty at the end of an expiration and thereby a reserve of air is kept. The diaphragm and abdominals are mostly free and involved in the respiratory activity. Now try this style of impeded breathing for a minute. Remember to keep your chest inflated throughout the inhalation-exhalation cycles.

Of these two disturbed patterns of breathing, the former one is the more effective in quelling excitement. The former pattern involves the maintaining of the *expirational attitude* and corresponds to a lack of aggressiveness in breathing. The person who breathes in this manner does not "take" the air from the environment, but breathes in a shy way. The latter pattern of breathing involves the maintaining of the *inspirational attitude*. By not allowing a full exhalation the person who is in this second style is not allowing a letting go or giving in. These patterns of breathing seem to correlate with other behaviors which are manifestations of the themes of not being aggressive and fear of giving in, respectively. In either case the unitary functioning of the body which is characteristic of natural breathing is lost, and whether out of shyness or the fear of letting go, sexual Arousal is dampened.

These disturbed patterns of breathing are effective means of interrupting the natural unfolding of the SCWC. An additional technique is simply to hold one's breath. Elegant in its simplicity, this is a frequently used emergency measure to rein in a sexual excitement which is gaining momentum.

There are additional methods for quelling excitement which can be used to augment the basic method, improper breathing. These include smoking, use of alcohol and other depressing drugs, poor nutrition, lack of exercise, lack of sufficient sleep and rest, and lack of play.

Smoking has an obvious role here. As the saturation of smoke in the air breathed increases, there is a lessening of oxygen available. In addition, the pathological changes in the lung tissue which are inevitable with prolonged smoking make the lungs less efficient in their task of oxygen uptake. I believe that the role of smoking in decreasing organismic Arousal is generally underestimated. In terms of the SCWC specifically, smoking is a method for taking the edge off the sexual excitement.

Use of various chemical agents also effectively lessens sexual Arousal. Using such drugs may be with the unconscious intention of avoiding sexual excitement, or the lowered excitement may be an unwanted side effect of taking a drug for some other purpose. The fact that people have individual responses to drugs and to dosages is beginning to be more widely recognized. Alcohol, of course, is traditionally in this society the most widely used and socially sanctioned of the tranquilizing drugs. For a pharmacologically nontechnical discussion of drugs which may affect sexual Arousal, I recommend the chapter "Drugs, Transference, and Sex" in *Night Thoughts*, by Avodah Offit (1981).

A lack of exercise, lack of sleep and rest, and lack of play all have a decidedly depressing effect on aliveness. Clearly, sexual Arousal is specifically affected. Exercise, sleep and rest, and play are highly interrelated. Play, most often, involves exercise. Sleep and rest support play and at the same time vigorous play leaves one ready for rest and sleep. Since this dynamic is recognized as aliveness, interference with these interrelated activities can diminish sexual aliveness at the point of Arousal. A less lively person will be less lively sexually.

What I have just written is so apparent as to be almost a truism, and yet it can be overlooked easily. I have marveled at times at the way patients have arranged to be tired whenever there was the "threat" of a sexual encounter. Perhaps the most common example of this is the couple who "try" to have sex only late at night after a long, hard day at work. Isn't it interesting how many people try to get "up for sex" only after they are "down for the night"?

So, as I see it, as each of these—exercise, sleep and rest, play—is neglected, sexual Arousal is potentially diminished.

I want to explore now the relationship between nutrition and sexual arousal. The question for us is, how can sexual arousal be diminished or avoided by means of eating? I see three patterns of eating which can alone or in combination lead to diminished excitement; they are overeating, undereating, and nonnutritious eating. I will cover these one at a time.

Sexual excitation can be directly interfered with by eating. As Reich (1980, p. 121) wrote, " . . . the compulsion to eat is a means of suppressing vegetative sensations in the abdomen." What Reich was writing about was the suppression of the bodily sensations of sexual Arousal through eating. As people learn to use eating as a way to avoid forbidden sexual sensations, a confusion may develop wherein the beginnings of sexual excitement may be mistaken for a need to eat. When eating then becomes a preferred mode of avoidance, the result is overeating. In this case eating follows from sex hunger in addition to a genuine food hunger based on nutritional needs. The usual result of this is obesity. Obesity and sexuality have long been related in the writings of psychoanalytic thinkers. This relationship has been supported clinically as well as elaborated theoretically. On a symbolic level the substitution of food for sex is apparent enough. Consider the parallels of "appetite," stimulation of orifice, ecstasy, and being full. And then there are the pleasant sensations of urination and defecation, made more frequent by the intake of increased food and drink. The parallel is acknowledged by a name given in the patois for oral sex — "eating."

Undereating is a less direct way of avoiding full sexual excitement. The key here is to eat so little as not to have a natural level of energy. The weakness which ensues from undereating will preclude a full sexual excitement.

Additionally, a pattern of chronic overeating or undereating can bring about a physical appearance which is less likely to attract sexual attention. So, by being "fat" or "skinny" one can decrease the likelihood of interactions which would be sexually arousing. (Here is a situation where Arousal is avoided by means of avoidance of Interaction. Remember the feedback loop in the SCWC whereby the Interaction could enhance the Arousal, three steps "upstream.")

Finally, there is nonnutritious eating. The dynamic is similar to one of the aspects of undereating, that of keeping one's energy store low. A person may do this without undereating, *per se*. The idea is to eat quantitatively enough, in terms of overall food intake, but to eat in a pattern which does not support an adequate and sustained level of energy. By missing certain nutrients in certain patterns one may attain a condition of low blood sugar and thereby a feeling of tiredness and lethargy. This will, of course, interfere with natural sexual Arousal. One technique is to skip meals, thereby going many hours without intake of nutrition.

So, overeating, undereating, and nonnutritious eating can be used alone or in concert to contribute to one's diminished sexual excitement.

Offit (1981, p. 165) has gone so far as to " . . . suspect that the majority of eating disorders result from sexual disorders." As I see it, the eating disorders are effective means of avoidance in the SCWC, specifically at the point of Arousal.

What I have presented in this chapter is an examination of the pathological dynamic of inhibiting or blocking the Arousal step in the SCWC. In response to the prohibition of sexual excitement demanded by a toxic sexual script there are several techniques. To not get "turned on" the following methods were submitted: avoid breathing, smoke several cigarettes, have a stiff drink or take a tranquilizer, stay tired, and have a hot fudge sundae at first hint of a sexual urge. For variety some variations of the basic techniques were discussed.

5. Sexual Deadening Through Clouded Awareness

The second pathological mechanism by which one can self-interrupt the SCWC is that of clouding awareness. No matter how sexually energized a person is, without the focusing of that energy by means of Awareness the likelihood of Satisfaction is almost nil. Awareness is the guide. Awareness involves the organismic "knowing" of what I want, what I am feeling, what I have to do in order to get what I want, with whom I have to do what it is I have to do to get what I want, and when I am satisfied and ready to withdraw. Clearly, Awareness is a process which extends throughout the entirety of a successful SCWC. The first half of the Contact Episode is designated the Awareness half because the sequence of Want → Arousal → Emotion is *primarily* a function of Awareness. However, Awareness is the process which underlies the Expression half of the Contact Episode (Action → Interaction → Satisfaction) as well as the Withdrawal Episode. The Expression

Episode is *secondarily* a function of Awareness; during Withdrawal, Awareness is again primary.

It is important to understand that "Awareness" is not just cognitive. It involves knowing through one's whole being. There is an old expression, "I can feel it in my bones." This saying captures the meaning of Awareness. As an organismic process, Awareness is another term for "consciousness."

Fritz Perls (1975) wrote that human existence is experienced along three dimensions. These are space, time, and awareness. The spatial dimension is a continuum from "there" to "here" and on to the opposite "there." The temporal dimension is a continuum from "then" (the past) to "now" (the present) and on to "then" (the future). Awareness, too, is a continuum which reaches from "not knowing" to "knowing." My existence is experienced in terms of these three converging parameters — I *am, here, now*. My "being," or "am-ness" is a function of the elaboration of my Awareness. (The recognition of these three dimensions is not original with Perls, and can be found in earlier philosophical writings. Perls, however, underscored them in his making them central to Gestalt therapy. They are found in his "principle of the here-and-now," and his use of the "awareness continuum." The explanation given here of these dimensions is my version.)

The specific processes which interfere with Awareness have been elaborated beautifully in the Gestalt therapy literature (Enright, 1970; Perls, 1947, 1969; Perls, 1973; Perls, Hefferline, and Goodman, 1951; Polster and Polster, 1973). I want to describe these several processes and then show how these apply specifically to my SCWC.

As I conceptualize the processes of clouding Awareness, I think of two subgroupings. First are the processes which create *confusion*. The second subgroup consists of those processes which are *dulling* of Awareness.

Awareness can be confused by means of the processes of introjection, projection, and confluence. What gets confused in each of these is ownership. For instance, in the case of introjection I believe that something is mine when it really is yours. That is, I have taken in your idea, value, belief, moral guideline, or so forth, and acted on it without having examined it thoroughly and decided if I really wanted to incorporate it into my overall system. The introject is like a piece of food swallowed whole. It has not been tasted, taken apart by chewing, and decided on, based on its taste. So, it has been swallowed whole or semiwhole and as such will not assimilate well. If toxic, this feature was missed by not tasting, and therefore it was not spit out.

Toxic introjects, as we have seen earlier, will poison the system. Even if not toxic, introjected material poses a problem in that in its unchewed (still structured) form it does not digest or assimilate completely. The result is indigestion, and sometimes regurgitation. So, coming back from our metaphor, introjected material is not assimilated into one's overall system of values, beliefs, and ideas. Therefore, introjects are not useful, and can cause much trouble as confusion ensues. Confusion is the primary symptom of introjection, since the introjector is acting on someone else's value, belief, or idea, and that material is not going to be consistent with and/or integrated with the introjector's overall ideology. A hallmark of introjection is verbatim quoting in a preaching or lecturing manner, again reflecting a lack of assimilation of the material.

Projection is the mirror image of introjection. With projection, again ownership is a confused issue, but in this case it is believing something is yours when actually it is mine. In projection I attribute an idea, belief, value or feeling to you when that material is mine.

Confluence, the third avenue to confused Awareness, involves a blurring of ego boundary such that I don't differentiate between "you" and "me," and recognize only "us." So, again, ownership is confused. In this case the idea, belief, value, feeling, or whatever is seen as "ours." Confluence can be recognized sometimes by the use of "we" or "us" when the meaning is "I" or "me."

Perls' (1973, p. 40–41) summarization of these three processes is as follows. "The introjector does as others would like him to do, the projector does unto others what he accuses them of doing to him, the man in pathological confluence doesn't know who is doing what to whom. . . ."

Awareness can also be clouded by means of processes of dulling. The dulling of Awareness is accomplished through deflection and through desensitization.

Deflection can be used by either the sender of a message or the receiver. In either case the message is diluted, and therefore the result is a dulling of Awareness. I cannot improve upon the statement made by Erv and Miriam Polster (1973, p. 89), so I quote them: "Deflection is a maneuver for turning aside from direct contact with another person ... by circumlocution, by excessive language, by laughing off what one says, by not looking at the person one is talking to, by being abstract rather than specific, by not getting the point, by coming up with bad examples or none at all, by politeness instead of directness, by stereotyped language rather than original language, by substituting mild emotions for intense ones, by talking *about* rather than talking *to*, and by shrugging off the importance of what one has said."

Desensitization refers to any dulling of Awareness by means of decreasing the acuity of a sensory modality. This includes visual blurring, tunnel vision, chronic "not hearing," frigidity, and general sensory dullness. These are probably the most common of the desensitizations, but any sensory modality may be chosen. Two methods of desensitization are possible. The first is a psychological process, and to which I have been referring. The second is a chemical process chosen for psychological reasons. So, for those who do not want to develop the skills of desensitization, breweries, distilleries, and pharmaceutical houses provide a vast array of products which can be put to this use with great effectiveness.

The processes for clouding Awareness are summarized in Figure 5.

In terms of the SCWC, the locations at which clouded Awareness is the primary mechanism of self-interruption are the following junctures: Withdrawal → Want, Arousal → Emotion, Interaction → Satisfaction, and Satisfaction → Withdrawal. Since there are four locations *where* the self-interruption is primarily a function of clouded Awareness I will take each one in turn and explore *what* problem is experienced and *why* the self-interruption is at that particular juncture. The *"how"* of clouded Awareness has been described.

When the self-interruption is between Withdrawal and Want, the problem experienced is low sexual interest. There are wide individual differences in the frequency of sexual desire, within what may be considered a normal range. What we are concerned with here, however, is the situation in which the person is stuck in

Figure 5. Processes for Interfering with Awareness

Clouded Awareness

Confused Awareness	*Dulled Awareness*
introjection	deflection
projection	desensitization
confluence	

the phase of Withdrawal for reasons which are not natural. This person may or may not recognize that the time spent in Withdrawal from sexual expression is unnaturally long. Sometimes this is passed off as just not being very interested in sex.

In other cases the person may report with concern that he or she is not feeling as sexually interested as he or she would like. The toxic script message which has been introjected in this situation is in essence, "Don't have sexual needs." The specific messages may vary from person to person, but the essence is as stated. In brief, the person who has the toxic message "Don't have sexual needs," will tend to self-interrupt the SCWC by staying inordinately long in Withdrawal, accomplishing this primarily by means of clouded Awareness. When the self-interruption is an inhibition, the person will lack in forcefulness. If the self-interruption is a complete block, then the person will remain in Withdrawal indefinitely.

A clouding of Awareness which effects a self-interruption between Arousal and Emotion can be quite complex. In fact, of the four loci where clouded Awareness is the primary mechanism of self-interruption, it is this one which takes the most forms. This is because two emotions, and their interactive blends, are involved. What this means in terms of introjected toxic script messages is the following: "Don't feel love," "Don't feel lust," and "Don't feel love with lust" (or "Don't feel lust with love"). To further complicate the scene, any one of those toxic script essences may be either a complete stopper (a block), or a diminisher of feeling (a degree of inhibition).

Taking the four essential toxic script messages one at a time, the "Don't feel love" message leaves the possessor with a fear of loving. This person is free to feel lust, but not love, so he or she may

be sexually active. What is lacking in all of that person's relationships is love, to some degree or another. Since loving is weak or
absent in relationships, often this person will "sexualize" all
relationships, in the sense of relating through lust or not at all. He
or she may interact with people for various practical reasons, but
person to person relating tends toward relating in terms of lustful
attraction. Sexual relating may be intense and exciting, but
tenderness and growing attachment will be diminished or absent.
This person may be able to "fuck," but not be good at "making
love."

When "Don't feel lust" is the toxic message, the script is a
platonic one. The person with this script may be very loving, and
may be able to express great affection through words and tender,
caring touch. What will be found lacking is the high energy, pas-
sionate sex. This person will be better at being affectionate than at
"making love," and "fucking" will be out of the question.

The two toxic script messages presented above are relatively
clear in their implications for behavior, even though they vary
greatly in degree depending on the severity of inhibition, or in the
extreme, the block. A bit more subtle in its manifestation is the next
toxic message which in its essence deals simultaneously with both
the feeling of love and of lust. The message here is that one cannot
combine love and lust, that these two sexual feelings are not to be
blended. The result is that if one feels loving towards another, he
or she cannot feel lustful. Conversely, with those towards whom
one feels lustful, he or she cannot feel loving.

The classic example of this problem is the man who loves his
wife, but is impotent with her, while able to have wild exciting sex,
being erectively potent, with a prostitute. The converse side of this
is being wildly lustful with someone, but declaring, "I could never
love her/him." Freud (1963) wrote at length about this situation in
a 1912 essay. In this essay he said that "To ensure a fully normal
attitude in love, two currents of feeling have to unite — we may
describe them as the tender affectionate feelings and the sensual
feelings . . . (p. 59)."

It was Freud's finding that "In only very few people of culture
are the two strains of tenderness and sensuality duly fused into one
(p. 64)." I do not know how prevalent this lack of fusion is today
as compared to Freud's 1912 Vienna. I do know that this condition

continues to exist, and in various degrees. As Freud noted in his essay, when love and lust are not fused, the object of one's lust is degraded. The person with whom one feels lustful is seen as beneath one, less than one's self.

In the case where both love and lust are allowed, but the toxic script message forbids the feeling of both of them with the same person, there are several possible manifestations which can be noticed. The person will have difficulty feeling love and lust for the same person, tending to have loving, platonic relationships with some people and lustful relationships with other people. The person will tend to elevate the loved people, making them more than they are, even placing them on a pedestal. The person will tend to degrade the people with whom he or she feels lust, even to the point of feeling contempt for them. The greater the inhibition for feeling love and lust fused, the greater the tendency to revere those who are loved and to hold in contempt those with whom one feels lust. With this script there is a tendency to regard others as saints or sinners, as love goddess or whore. In very subtle form the split in objects of love and lust may be a split between the literal person and the person in one's fantasy. So, sex with one's partner may be made tolerable by a fantasized sexual encounter with a person towards whom one can feel the other sexual emotion.

In each of these situations the step from Arousal to Emotion has been interfered with by means of Awareness which is not fully developed. The result is that love and lust are not fully experienced in their combined form, necessary for ultimate Satisfaction in the SCWC.

The next juncture at which clouded Awareness is the primary mechanism of self-interruption in the SCWC is between Interaction and Satisfaction. This is a very subtle transition, and one which is sometimes overlooked by writers on sexuality. The point is, however, that no matter how well one has progressed through the SCWC, this only becomes an accomplishment to the extent that Satisfaction is the result. Not only does Satisfaction mean that the sexual tension previously felt has been resolved, it means that what one has done has been successful. The second point is that one's behavior is validated by the experience of Satisfaction. The experience of Satisfaction carries the meaning that the steps taken up to that point were effective, or valid. The transition from a potentially satisfying Action → Interaction sequence to Satisfaction is carried by high level organismically based Awareness. This Awareness can be clouded by a toxic introject which in essence demands "Don't enjoy sex!" The variations on this theme include "Don't be sexually satisfied," and "Don't be competent at sex," these more specific toxic script messages corresponding to the tension resolution and the validational components of Satisfaction. The possessor of such a toxic introject is likely to complain that sex is not as enjoyable as he or she would like, that after sex he or she feels unfulfilled, or that "something" was missing.

It is this inhibition or block to Satisfaction which is a major component of what I discussed in Chapter 1 as lack of orgastic potency. Low orgastic potency is contributed to by all of the mechanisms which interrupt the SCWC, but this particular clouding of awareness is of great impact. Satisfaction means that sexual tension has been successfully resolved, and that, as may be recalled from Chapter 1, is a hallmark of orgastic potency. So, a toxic introject which demands that one not enjoy sex is demanding that one not give in fully to orgasm. Such a person will have weak orgasms, if at all.

The final juncture in the SCWC where clouded Awareness is the primary impediment to a natural flow is between Satisfaction and Withdrawal. The toxic introject which is at work here at first seems not to oppose sexuality. Its essence is "Don't let go, you may not get another chance." So, it may seem to be in support of sexual satisfaction. What it does not support, and in fact forbids, is the natural rhythm of sexuality. The natural rhythm is one of coming together and going apart, for it is only by going apart that the sexual need/tension is allowed to develop. And, it is that need/tension which is the psychobiological ground for sexuality. The natural paradox is that separation follows Satisfaction, not continued contact.

By "hanging on" to the contact after Satisfaction is complete, the contact will move to being irrelevant and if continued even longer it will become noxious. The problem which manifests when one possesses such a sexual script is either an apparent insatiability or a quality of ruining what would have been satisfying had it been stopped sooner. This person may seem never to get enough in the sexual encounter, wanting more and more. If this is continued very long, the satisfaction which might have been felt is converted into an experience of aversion.

I want to emphasize, again, that clouding of Awareness is involved in a self-interruption at any juncture of the SCWC. All self-interruptions of the SCWC are in response to a toxic introject, and introjection is one of the ways of clouding Awareness, more specifically, of confusing Awareness. In addition to the confusion of Awareness brought about by a toxic introject, the clouding may be augmented by the other methods of confusing Awareness and the methods of dulling Awareness. I identified the clouding of Awareness as *the* means of self-interruption at four specific junctures in the SCWC. The other three junctures each has a specific mechanism for self-interruption which I designate as primary, even though its existence is in response to an underlying toxic introject. Thus, in Chapter 4 I explored the quieting of Arousal as the primary mechanism of self-interruption between Want and Arousal. In the two chapters following the present one I will explore the two remaining pathological mechanisms.

Before leaving the topic of clouded Awareness as a pathological mechanism, I want to give an example of how the methods of confusion and dulling can augment one another. I will create a hypothetical example in order to employ all of the methods at once.

Imagine a young man who complains that he doesn't seem to have much sexual interest. He forgets to have sex for weeks at a time, until reminded by his young wife. When reminded, he reports that he initiates sex by asking her, but that she really isn't very interested either. He concludes that "We don't seem to have much need for sex in our marriage. But we are missing something."

This situation could result from the following sources of clouded Awareness, revealed over several in-depth interviews:

(1) When he was a boy his mother scolded him for   *Confused*
     "playing with himself" and told him that boys   *Awareness*
     don't have to do things like that. As a preteen his
     father gave him a "man-to-man" lecture in which
     he said "It's weak to need a woman. A strong man
     can get along without having sex." (*Toxic intro-
     ject*: Don't have sexual needs!)

(2) He "asks" for sex by saying, "Well, I guess we'd   *Dulled*
     better fool around sometime soon." (*Deflection*   *Awareness*
     of the message sent.)

(3) She responds with, "Yes, like how about now?" He   *Dulled*
     doesn't quite hear her, hearing instead, "Yes, but   *Awareness*
     now?" (*Desensitization.*)

(4) So he says, "Well, maybe tomorrow night." She   *Dulled*
     says, again, "How about now?" He laughs, looks   *Awareness*
     away, and replies, "That's very considerate of you,
     but I can wait." (*Deflection* of message received
     and message sent.)

(5) While lying in the dark in bed he thinks to   *Confused*
     himself, "She really doesn't want to have sex."   *Awareness*
     (*Projection.*)

(6) Before falling asleep he concludes, "We are   *Confused*
     making it without sex; we really don't need it   *Awareness*
     much." (*Confluence.*)

With this vignette a considerable tangle has already been pro-
duced. And we have not even explored the wife's side! The vignette
is typical, and shows how each method of confusing and dulling
awareness combines in synergy to support the operation of the
original introjection. And so, a tangle of confluence, projection,
deflection of messages sent, deflection of messages received, and
desensitization. All of this to maintain obedience to an introjected
message, a message from the father and the mother, which was in
essence, "Don't have sexual needs!"

6. Sexual Deadening Through Retroflection of Action

Having covered the first two of the pathological mechanisms for self-interrupting the SCWC (quieting Arousal and clouding Awareness), we can turn our attention to the third and fourth mechanisms, both of which involve "retroflection." These latter two mechanisms are focused on the expression of sexual energy, or the Action → Interaction sequence. The nonenactment of sexual energy involves the processes of "retroflection of Action" and "retroflection of Interaction" (Smith, 1985). The subject of the present chapter is the former, retroflection of Action.

Retroflection of Action, as is implied, is focused on the juncture between Emotion and Action, with the purpose of preventing Action from taking place.

Drawing on Kierkegaard's writing on the relation of the self to the self, Perls (1969) recognized retroflection as a process in which the self acts upon itself. It is as if there is an active self and a passive self, with the active self doing something to the passive self. In the

63

case of retroflection of Action, the active self acts in such a way as to negate or neutralize the part of the self which has an urge toward forbidden Action, thereby rendering that part of the self passive.

What I have termed "retroflection of Action" is what Perls (1947, 1969) referred to as "self-control." With self-control there is an inhibition or a block to Action, and in the present context we are looking at this in terms of a self-interruption in the SCWC. In other words, I am distinguishing self-control or retroflection of Action as self-discipline in a positive sense from the negative sense whereby the natural SCWC is interrupted. Perls (1947, 1969) suggested that most people understand self-control to mean repression of spontaneous needs and the compulsion to do things without being genuinely interested in doing them. Such repression of spontaneous need is the perverse use of self-control.

John Enright (1970, p. 112) addressed this form of retroflection as follows. "Retroflection describes the general process of negating, holding back, or balancing the impulse tension by additional, opposing sensorimotor tension.... [T]he net result of all this canceled-out muscular tension is zero — no overt movement...." Enright went on to point out that chronic retroflection, of the type he described, is what Reich (1949) had earlier identified by the term "character armor." Reich also used the term "muscular armor." The idea is that when muscles are held in chronic tension in order to neutralize the forbidden impulse, the body becomes hard in the area where this process is taking place. Thus, it is as if the muscles become an armor, there is created a "body armor."

Perls (1947, 1969, p. 229) had the following to say about this action-deadening form of retroflection. "We repress vital functions (vegetative energy, as Reich calls their sum) by muscular contractions. The civil war raging in the neurotic organism is mostly waged between the motoric system and unaccepted organismic energies which strive for expression and gratification. The motoric system has to a great extent lost its function as a working, active world-bound system and, by retroflection, has become the jailer rather than the assistant of important biological needs."

In the case of the SCWC, retroflected Action interrupts the flow between feeling the sexual emotions and taking action on these feelings. This is of special interest because it is the transition point between the Awareness portion and the Expression portion of the

Contact Episode. It is at this transition point that the musculoskeletal system becomes of primary focus. During the Awareness portion of the Contact Episode the major activity is in the brain and vegetative nervous system, but with the transition to Action, the musculoskeletal system is activated. For many people it is exactly this transition which is problematic.

Especially with well-educated people, I have found clinically that recognition of sexual urges, sexual arousal, and even experiencing the emotions of sex may be permissible, but the expression of sexuality is what is forbidden. I recall a line from a popular song of some years ago, "You can't go to jail for what you're thinking." The refrain of the song is "Standing on the corner watching all the girls go by." That song captured the essence of the self-interruption between Awareness and Expression, namely, sex is safe as long as you don't do anything about it.

While touching on the essence of this locus of self-interruption, it seems appropriate to make explicit the toxic introject which would be operating. Although the specific toxic script may take many variations on this theme, the essential theme is "Don't act (sexually)!" This means that with this toxic sexual script operating, without additional ones, the possessor is free to recognize sexual urges, become sexually aroused, and feel love and lust. Such a person may, then, be open to sexually stimulating sights and sounds. He or she may enjoy looking at attractive, even provocative people, and even talking flirtatiously. But as "turned on" as such a person feels, the toxic message interferes with a flow into the doing of sex.

It is interesting to see how specific the "Don't act (sexually)" message can be. The message may define "acting sexually" as genital to genital contact, thereby leaving other activity unrestricted. Or, at the other extreme, it may include in its definition any exposure of genitals and female breasts to touch or even to view. In this extreme even looking at another's genitals or breasts may be construed to be sexual activity. Very often there is a hierarchy of sexual activity which is used, with the prohibition being at a certain level. The toxic introject may define the conditions under which different levels of the hierarchy may be engaged in without anxiety and guilt. Let's take a hypothetical example. A particular individual may have a hierarchy as follows:

Holding hands	If you like the other person.
Kissing	If you have gone out more than once.
Necking	If you are dating each other exclusively.
Touching breasts	If you are in love.
Touching genitals	If you are engaged to be married.
Intercourse in missionary position	If you are married.
Intercourse in other positions	Never.
Oral-genital sex	Never.
Other	(Didn't know there is anything else.)

(Keep in mind that this is a hierarchy set up by an introjected toxic message, not a hierarchy derived from assimilated experience.) The possessor of this hierarchy may act on sexual feelings, but the activity which is allowed is rigidly set and absolute with respect to the arbitrary categories of relationship stated. There is no allowance there for spontaneity, experimentation, and the flexibility of an evolving sexual code.

My observation is that with adults the introjected message "Don't act (sexually)" most often means "Don't have intercourse." With that message one may do "everything but" and still not violate the toxic introject. As long as there is not penetration, "it doesn't count."

And, now to get oriented again. The self-interruption in the SCWC which we are exploring is at the junction of Emotion → Action. This is *where* the problem is. *Why* at this juncture? Because of a toxic introject which states "Don't act (sexually)!" The next step is to delve more deeply into *how* this self-interruption is brought about.

So far my description of retroflection of Action as a pathological mechanism has not dealt specifically with the realm of sexuality. To that, I want to turn now. The basic sexual action is the pelvic thrust. It is that rocking motion of the pelvis which accomplishes the primary, paradigmatic sexual union. Other sexual contacts add richness and variety, but it is pelvic Action which is basic in sexual union. Therefore the pelvis is the bodily site of retroflected Action in the SCWC.

The mechanical basis for retroflection is the antagonistic arrangement of muscles. A muscle can only contract and relax, it cannot exert force by extending itself. As a muscle relaxes it can be extended by the contraction of its antagonist. Consider, for instance, the arm. The arm bends as the biceps contracts and the triceps relaxes. So, the biceps and triceps are the "prime movers" of arm bending and extending, and are antagonists. Other muscles help by stabilizing, hence "stabilizers," and by aiding in the movement. The latter are called "synergists." Completing the example, stabilizing muscles in the shoulder keep the arm in place as it is bent and straightened. At the same time, synergists in the forearm contribute to the bending when the arm is in certain positions. When there is retroflection of Action, the forbidden Action is frozen by using the antagonist to counter and balance the muscle which would be the prime mover for that movement. More accurately, several antagonists would work in symphony to oppose the prime mover, and the synergists and fixation muscles, in order to stop a complex movement.

The pelvis is activated by a complex array of muscles. For simplicity, we can think of the thrusting of the pelvis as involving primarily the abdominal muscles and the muscles of the lower back. For our purposes here it is not necessary to be technical about the pelvic musculature. So, think of the abdominal muscles contracting and the muscles of the lower back relaxing as the pelvis rocks or thrusts forward, and the muscles of the lower back contracting and the abdominal muscles relaxing as the pelvis rocks backward. These two sets of muscles are the prime movers in pelvic rocking and thrusting. Other muscles are involved in stabilization and in synergic activity. Since the lower back muscles and the abdominal muscles are antagonists, the failure of either to relax effectively dampens the body movement caused by the contraction of the other. This is how pelvic activity is dampened or stopped in this primary, paradigmatic sexual form.

Other muscles of the pelvis, and its extensions, the legs, can also contribute to the retroflection of sexual Action. The adductors of the legs, those muscles on the inside of the thighs which bring the legs together, can remain tense. This makes the spreading of the legs difficult or painful. Such tensing keeps the genitals from being fully exposed and especially in women makes genital contact more difficult. Interestingly, these thigh adductors have been called the "morality muscles." A tensing of the hip muscles, including those which work antagonistically with the adductors, greatly diminishes pelvic motility. Less dramatically, but still with effect, a tensing of the legs will dampen pelvic movement. This is true for the thighs, hamstrings, and even the calves. A particular site of tension which may not be associated easily with sexual movements is the feet. When the feet are tensed, toes made stiff either in extended or contracted position, the pelvis can be affected. Clinical experience bears this out. The point here is that tension in the legs or feet has a dampening effect on pelvic movement. The reason is simply that many of the leg muscles attach to the pelvic bones. The legs are attached to the pelvis and so when they are not relaxed the pelvis cannot move freely without them. With tense legs, the appendages are carried with the pelvis through its excursion, rather than there being a free, hinging movement. I am reminded of the old gospel song in which the truth is sung, as "the hip bone's connected to the leg bone...."

So, a freely moving pelvis requires hinging from above and from below. This requires antagonistic coordination of the abdominal and lower back muscles, and relaxed leg muscles, respectively.

Another category of muscles which may be held rigid and thereby interfere with sexual activity are the muscles of the genitals and anus. Perhaps best known is spasm of the muscles at the opening of the vagina, making penetration painful and difficult, if not impossible. Other muscles may be less dramatic in their effect, but still can perform a function of interference. A tightening of the urinary or anal sphincters is an example. It has been suggested that being what in the vernacular is sometimes called "uptight" may correlate highly with a tight anal sphincter. The vernacular offers another phrase which may be the recognition of this correlation, namely "tight assed." And indeed, it can be demonstrated that a tense sphincter diminishes the sexual experience.

Retroflected Action can be recognized by observing the body. In its mildest form the retroflection is physically manifested in a holding back, so that sexual movement is weak, diminished, or awkward. Such weakness or awkwardness comes from the sexual ambivalence, manifested on the muscular level. The sexual urge and the sexual prohibition are fighting, so there is a simultaneous reaching out and holding back. Sexual expansion and contraction against sexual expansion compete. As the body is divided against itself, its performance must be weak or awkward.

In moderate form, a retroflection of sexual Action manifests as tightness or stiffness. Some one, or more often, some combination of the muscles involved have a lack of flexibility when sexual activity is entered into. This phenomenon has been described in this way by Joseph Zinker (1977, p. 26), "In retroflection, the person tightens a part of himself, rather than using that part to express a feeling in the direction of other people." The key to distinguishing this moderate level of retroflected Action is that the muscular stiffness occurs on the occasion of sexual activity.

True muscular armor is the severe form of retroflected Action. The tightness is chronic and not limited to times of sexual activity. As Reich (1949, p. 349) stated, " . . . in the case of . . . armoring, the muscular rigidity is chronic and automatic."

In addition to the above, retroflected sexual Action may be identified by a number of experienced body phenomena. Enright (1970, p. 112) suggested that " . . . since there is increased activity at the point of muscular opposition, awareness may develop there as pain or discomfort." Similarly, Zinker (1977, p. 103) has written that "The retroflector usually suffers physical (musculoskeletal) symptoms which show where the energy is frozen." The idea, here, is that physical discomfort *may* be a symptom of retroflected Action. A working hypothesis derived from this view has been offered by Patricia Baumgardner (1975, p. 16): " . . . any discomfort not induced by disease or trauma is indicative of and the result of unexpressed feeling." This means, for example, that a pain in the lower back which cannot be accounted for by a recent physical trauma such as a fall or by a disease process such as a kidney infection, may be hypothesized to be the symptom of retroflection of sexual Action.

There are, of course, degrees of severity of physical discomfort which may be experienced because of retroflection of sexual Action. I have taken a lead from something which Perls, Hefferline, and

Goodman (1951, p. 162) wrote in reference to retroflection, "The end result of such censoring, whether recognized or not, is invariably a more or less psychosomatic dysfunction: impairment of powers of orientation, or manipulation, ache, weakness, or even degeneration of tissues." That final phrase, "degeneration of tissues," deserves some exploration, for its implications are far reaching. For one thing, this suggests a revision of the above quoted material by Baumgardner. The revision would acknowledge that any discomfort not induced by physical trauma may be the direct result of unexpressed feeling, or the symptom of a disease process which may have been brought about in part or in whole through unexpressed feeling. A degenerative disease may come directly from the withholding of feeling and an infectious disease may be contributed to by the withholding of feeling.

Let me explain this last statement. With severe retroflection of sexual Action there is an abnormal mechanical stress placed on the joints, the muscles, and the connecting tissues of the sexual apparatus. This may lead directly to degeneration of the hard and soft tissues in question. The rigidity of physical structure may mechanically interfere with the normal flow of blood, lymph, and nerve impulses within the pelvic segment. This same rigidity may also mechanically interfere with the specific sexual functioning of the sexual apparatus in terms of the flow of fluids. In addition, there may be a shift to prolonged dominance of the sympathetic portion of the autonomic nervous system with the attending tissue and hormonal manifestations. The result is a lowering of the vitality of the pelvic segment. This is synonymous with degenerative disease. The pelvic segment, in this state of lowered vitality, is thereby vulnerable to invasion by pathogens. The immune system of the body may be lowered in its strength, and the pelvic segment in particular may be vulnerable to infection.

Even though the sexual Action is diminished in retroflection, physical work is being performed by the opposing muscles. With retroflection of Action it is as if one were doing isometric exercises, and when this becomes chronic as in muscular armoring, it is perpetual isometric contractions without rest. This muscular activity, of course, brings with it certain physiological demands — increased supply of oxygen and nutrients and increased removal of waste products. So, even with *retroflected* Action, an increased demand is made on the cardiovascular system, the lymph system, the respiratory system, the endocrine system, and so forth. At the same time, the normal movements which correlate with these increased demands are absent. So, the body as a whole is in a very unnatural state when sexual Action is chronically retroflected.

A point which I have touched upon, and perhaps not made explicit enough, is that body armoring involves *segments* of the body, not just a particular muscle or muscle group. The segment is a functional unit including viscera. As Reich (1949, p. 371) stated this himself, "Armor segments, then, comprise those organs and muscle groups which are in functional contact with each other, which can induce each other to participate in expressive movement."

I suggest at this point that the reader go back to Chapter 2 and review the last few pages in which the neuroendocrinal dynamics that attend contraction against sexual expansion are discussed. That material adds a dimension to understanding the retroflection of Action in the pelvic segment.

I have called attention in this chapter to three forms of retroflection of sexual Action. These vary in their severity from weak or awkward action, to body stiffness or tightness, to pelvic armoring. Much of the material which I have presented is hypothetical. It is consistent with a great deal of clinical observation by many people, some of which I have quoted. I will extend this speculation one step more.

At the level of weak or awkward action there may be an experience of heat. That may be throughout the pelvic segment, or it may be focused in a particular spot. The hot spot suggests an accumulation of high energy in that body area without its release through full processing. As the body area becomes energized, but that energy is not afforded full expression, it is converted into static heat.

Moving to the next level, that of stiffness or tightness, there may be painful areas or cold areas. Pain can follow from the prolonged tensing of the muscles, either as muscle fatigue or cramping of the muscles. Such pain tends to occur in a specific area of the pelvic segment, rather than to be generalized. The blood supply or energy flow may be impeded by the prolonged tensing of the muscles, with resulting cold spots. Frequently, when there is a cold spot in the pelvic segment because of this dynamic, there will be a hot spot elsewhere in the body. As the pelvis, as a whole, or some specific spot within the pelvic segment becomes "undercharged" with energy (cold), that energy may be displaced to another body area which then becomes "overcharged" with energy (hot). This often shows up as a flushing of the face during a potentially sexually arousing experience.

At the extreme level of retroflected sexual Action, body armoring, a variety of symptoms may manifest. With the extreme chronicity of muscle tensing found at this level there may be a chronic aching in muscles, joints, or viscera. In time this aching may evolve into numbness, a deadness of the pelvic segment or some part thereof. In addition, there may be the aches, pains, or other manifestations of degenerative disease if such develops. These symptoms vary widely and may include, for example, menstrual dysfunction (amenorrhea, dysmenorrhea), prostatic discharge, and abnormal growths, malignant or nonmalignant. (For a detailed exposition on the theory of cancer as a result of body armor I call your attention to Reich's 1973 book *The Cancer Biopathy*.) High susceptibility to infectious diseases of the pelvic region, such as yeast infections, urethritis and prostatitis, may also result from the low vitality of a heavily armored pelvic segment.

Remember, a self-interruption in the SCWC may be either an inhibition or a block. Relating this distinction to the three forms of retroflected sexual Action, the first two represent levels of inhibition. With the first, Weak or Awkward Action, there is Action, but in a diminished form. Again, with the second form, Body Stiffness or Tightness, there is Action, but in an even more diminished form. Body Armor, too, may allow some Action, but with this form of retroflected sexual Action the inhibition may be severe or there may even be a complete block. That is, with a severe armoring of the pelvis, all sexual Action may be arrested.

I offer Figure 6 as a summary of the forms and symptoms of retroflection of sexual action.

To review, what I have dealt with in the present chapter is as follows. *Where* the problem is, is at the junction between Emotion and Action in the SCWC. The reason *why* the self-interruption is at that particular site is because of a toxic introject which says, in essence, "Don't act (sexually)!" *How* the self-interruption is

Figure 6. Forms and Symptoms
of Retroflection of Sexual Action

I. Weak or Awkward
Action: (Inhibition)

Weak pelvic movement.
Clumsy or awkward
pelvic movement. Hot
spots in the pelvic seg-
ment.

II. Body Stiffness or
Tightness: (Inhibition)

Stiffness or tightness in
the pelvic segment.
Painful area in the
pelvic segment.
Cold spots in the pelvic
segment.

III. Body Armor
(Inhibition or Block)

Extreme muscle tension
in the pelvic segment.
Aches in the pelvic
segment.
Numbness in the pelvic
segment.
Degenerative disease of
the reproductive
system (menstrual
problems, abnormal
growths, prostatic
enlargement, low
sperm count, etc.).*
Proneness to infectious
diseases of the sexual
apparatus (yeast
infections, prostatitis,
urethritis, etc.).*

Continuum of Increasing Severity and Chronicity

*These conditions are not proven to be the result of pelvic armoring. This material is speculative, based on theory and limited clinical evidence. These conditions may occur for reasons other than pelvic armoring.

accomplished is by means of retroflection of Action, which can take one of three forms: Weak or awkward action, Body stiffness or tightness, or Body armoring. Inhibition is more pronounced as one moves from the first to the second, and from the second to the third, with the retroflection of Action reaching its limit as a block in the extreme case of body armoring. Finally, *what* the problem is is a lack of sexual movement. The symptoms may include weakness of sexual movement, clumsiness, awkwardness of sexual movement, stiffness of the pelvis, hot spots or cold spots in the pelvic region, aches, pains or numbness in the pelvic structures. Secondary symptoms may ensue as result of degenerative disease or infectious disease proneness following from the state of low vitality of a severely armored pelvis.

7. Sexual Deadening Through Retroflection of Interaction

And, now, the fourth pathological mechanism for interrupting the SCWC, retroflection of Interaction. As is revealed in its name, this mechanism provides an interruption between the Action and Interaction stages of the SCWC. What this means is that sexual expression is not fully allowed to become interactive with a target person who would provide the possibility of sexual Satisfaction. Sexual activity in this situation meets a partially or wholly solipsistic fate. The essence of retroflected sexual Interaction is the absence, total or partial, of a sexual partner.

Writing about this form of retroflection, which I have designated "retroflection of interaction" (Smith, 1985), the Polsters (1973, p. 71) said, "The *retroflector* abandons any attempt to influence his environment by becoming a separate and self-sufficient unit, reinvesting his energy back into an exclusively intrapersonal system and severely restricting the traffic between himself and the environment." In a similar vein Perls, Hefferline,

75

and Goodman (1951, p. 146) stated of the retroflector that "He stops directing various energies outward in attempts to . . . satisfy his needs; instead he . . . *substitutes himself in place of the environment* as the target of behavior. To the extent that he does this, he splits his personality into 'doer' and 'done to.'" This last statement is of particular importance in understanding the dynamics of retroflected interaction, the fact that the person is both the actor and the target of her or his own action.

Upon closer examination it becomes clear that there are two forms of retroflection of Interaction. Early in his writing Perls made this explicit. Following a discussion of how one may make herself or himself the target of something which he or she would more appropriately direct toward another, Perls, Hefferline, and Goodman (1951, p. 150) noted, "Retroflections also include what one *wanted from* others but was unsuccessful in obtaining, with the outcome that now, for want of anyone else to do it, one gives it to himself." Somewhat later, the Polsters (1973, p. 82) again drew attention to this distinction: "Retroflection is a hermaphroditic function wherein the individual turns back against himself what he would like *to do to someone else,* or does to himself what he would like *someone else to do to him.*"

Let us turn now specifically to the sexual realm. Since natural sexual behavior involves both the doing of things sexual and the receiving of things sexual, both forms of retroflected Interaction can be brought to bear. One can both be sexual *toward oneself* instead of toward another, and can receive sex *from oneself* instead of from another.

A point of clarification is in order here, I believe, concerning natural and unnatural instances of retroflection of sexual Interaction. In the discussion which follows, the focus will be on retroflection of Interaction as a mechanism for self-interruption in the SCWC, that is, a pathological use of retroflection of Interaction. To direct sexual energies toward oneself is certainly not pathological *per se.* Recall, for instance, the long discussion of masturbation in Chapter 1, in which I elaborated my view of the role of autoeroticism in one's overall profile of sexual aliveness. I do not wish to be redundant here so I will not restate that discussion. Suffice it to say that lust turned inward can be of great value, and love turned inward is a necessity for living well. The problem is when the Actions stemming from love and lust are chronically turned inward as an avoidance of sexual Interaction. (I suggest at this point a rereading of the first several pages of Chapter 1 to allow an integration of that material on masturbation with the present material on pathological retroflection of sexual Interaction.)

Since the retroflector of sexual Interaction plays both the role of "doer" and "done to," it would be difficult to recognize by the behavior alone which form of retroflection of Interaction was occurring. Is an act of self-stroking a case of doing to oneself what one would like to do to another, or is it a case of doing to oneself what one would like for another to do to one? The answer, I believe, must come from the person performing the act, through conscientious introspection. The behaviors may include self-complimenting, statements of liking and loving oneself, self-holding, self-patting, self-stroking, self-preening, and masturbation in all of its diverse forms.

The loss here is that by making oneself the target of one's sexual activity, the "doer" fails to have the experience of sexually loving another, and the "done to" fails to have the experience of being sexually loved by another. The system is a closed one. Rather than two energy fields interacting, with the synergistic building of intensity, only one energy field exists. As Zinker (1977, p. 103) expressed this loss, "The price he pays — among other things — is that of using his own energy rather than being replenished by another person."

The obvious instance of retroflection of sexual Interaction is where sex is enacted in solitude. Where no partner is literally present, there is a Block in sexual Interaction. At the deepest level of retroflected sexual Interaction, not only is there no literal partner, but a sexual partner is not even allowed into the fantasy realm. The person who is "really into" herself or himself sexually will have masturbatory sex without fantasizing a partner.

This may be a clue to extreme fear of other people. Still at a Blocked level, but not as severe, is the situation of sexual activity without a literal partner, but with a fantasized partner. In this situation there is a powerful element of safety in that the person has control of the partner who is but a figment of her or his imagination. Moving beyond the Blocks to sexual Interaction, there is also a level of Inhibition. In the case of Inhibition, there is a literal sexual partner present. As long as a literal partner is present and

Figure 7. Levels of Retroflected
Sexual Interaction

Increasing	(Inhibition)	Sexual activity with a partner while fantasizing about another.
Levels	(Block)	Sexual activity without a partner while fantasizing about someone.
of		
Retroflection	(Block)	Sexual activity without a partner and without fantasizing about anyone.

sexual Action is not Blocked, the avenue for literal, concrete Interaction is open.

The need for partial retroflection (Inhibition) of sexual Interaction can be met in this situation by means of fantasizing a different partner. So, as sex is literally enacted with one person, it is enacted with someone else in fantasy. This is a situation in which, to use a colloquial phrase, one's "heart is not in it." By fantasizing of another partner, one is retroflecting some of the sexual Interaction from the literal partner present. The fantasy partner is in one's own mind. He or she is a figment of one's imagination. (I suggest a rereading of the material on the role of fantasy in sex found in Chapter 1.) These levels of retroflection of sexual Interaction are summarized in Figure 7.

And now the question arises, why self-interrupt at this particular juncture in the SCWC? The answer, of course, resides in the toxic introject which is operating. If the toxic message is essentially, "Don't be sexual *with anyone!*", then the sexual script calls for self-interruption between the stages of Action and Interaction. Depending on the severity of the message, both in terms of the content itself and the catastrophic threat, the person is led into an inhibition or a block in her or his freedom to be sexual with another person.

Sometimes the toxic message is more specific and stipulates a particular class of people with whom one is forbidden to be sexually interactive. When this is the case, the person in question may sexually engage well with others outside the stipulated class, but experience an inhibition or block if sex is attempted with someone identified as not allowable. The class can be identified in almost any manner in the statement of the toxic message. One interesting example is the message to the young man, "Don't be sexual *with girls!*" If this message is introjected and taken quite literally, the young man may find a loophole which would allow sexual Interaction with other males. If heterosexual Interaction is specifically forbidden and homosexual Interaction is not, then homosexual Interaction may be the Interaction of choice.

Another example, and one which I have worked with clinically, is a situation where a couple have been sexually active before marrying, but upon marrying one of the couple becomes much less sexually interactive. He or she may prefer masturbation, or find herself or himself engaging in a great deal of fantasy of other partners while having sex with the spouse. I am not dealing here with the staleness which can ensue after a long exclusive sexual relationship, but rather an abrupt and dramatic shift which coincides with marriage. The message which is operating here is essentially "Don't be sexual *with someone that you're married to!* That is too serious." Before marriage, sex was fun, playful, perhaps even frivolous. But sex in marriage may be defined as "heavy," "serious," and an acknowledgment of nigh-on inescapable commitment, or, a "burden." A variation on this theme is the script message, "Don't be sexual *with anyone you know* (or like, or are friends with)!" Again, the script message is completed by some additional statement that "this is too serious" in some respect.

Sometimes there is a toxic message which is common in a culture or a subculture. The result is a toxic cultural script. I offer an example of such a toxic cultural script which applies to sexual Interaction with a particular category of person. The toxic message is "Don't be sexual *with a menstruating woman!*" To the possessor of this message, this means that he may be sexually interactive with the woman in question when she is not menstruating, but during her period sexual interaction is forbidden. Such a man experiences a block or an inhibition of his sexuality in the presence of an otherwise appropriate partner when she is menstruating. The catastrophic expectation which has accompanied the content of this toxic cultural sexual script has varied, but in essence has promised dire consequences to the man who failed to heed the warning. Behind this threat has been the belief that women are dirty, dangerous, or irrational while menstruating. Menstruation, itself, has been termed "the curse." There is biblical support for this view that the menses are a punishment and the womb a source of evil. For example, in Leviticus 15:19 it is proclaimed:

> When a woman has a discharge of blood which is her regular discharge from her body, she shall be in her impurity . . . and whoever touches her shall be unclean. . . . And if any man lies with her, and her impurity is on him, he shall be unclean . . . and every bed on which he lies shall be unclean.

As late as the 1950s there were scientists attempting to demonstrate the existence of "meno-toxins" given off by menstruating women, which, if injected, would kill plants and laboratory rats (Offit, 1981).

These are but a few of the examples of possible specific classes of persons which can be excluded, by a toxic introjected message, from one's sexual Interaction. Excluded, that is, from unblocked and uninhibited sexual activity. In other cases, as has been mentioned, the exclusion is more general, making full interactional sexuality with anyone difficult, if not impossible, without severe conflict.

I want to summarize at this point. In the present chapter I have dealt with retroflection of Interaction in the SCWC as a mechanism of self-interruption. This is the *how* of self-interruption which occurs at the Action → Interaction juncture. The way this manifests is as a diminishing or complete stopping of sexual Interaction. This is the *what* of the problem. Having indicated the what, the where, and the how of the issue, the last question is *why*. The reason is the presence of a toxic introject which in essence says, "Don't be sexual *with anyone!*" (or with some specific class of persons).

This concept of retroflecting one's love rather than sharing it with another is an ancient one, and the basis for one of the minor classic myths. The myth of Narcissus is a portrayal of a love self-directed, a love turned back on the lover rather than given to another being. Classic myths such as this one have endured centuries of telling and reading. Their appeal, which endures profoundly, seems to lie in their encapsulating of the basic and universal themes of human experience. That is, to use a term of Carl

Jung, they give life to archetypal themes. As the myth is listened to, if it is indeed heard, the person hearing it will experience some psychic resonance with the archetypal theme. The hearer recognizes the archetype, as only can happen when something forgotten is reintroduced. Hence, the "re-cognition." Jung believed that there is a "collective unconscious" which is the basis for this recognition when an archetype is presented. Applying this line of thought to the myth of Narcissus, the suggestion is that we all resonate with its theme, recognizing in ourselves at least the potential for making ourselves the sole object of our love.

Here is how the myth of Narcissus goes. Narcissus was a beautiful lad, so beautiful that all of the girls who saw him longed to be his. Narcissus, however, wanted none of them. Regardless of how beautiful she might have been, none could turn his head. Eventually, one of the smitten damsels prayed to the gods for Narcissus to be appropriately dealt with. Nemesis, clever goddess of righteous anger, performed her magic. For, as Narcissus bent over a limpid pool to satisfy his thirst, he saw his reflection and fell in love with it. "Now I know," said he, "what others have suffered from me, for I burn with love of my own self — and yet how can I reach that loveliness I see mirrored in the water? But I cannot leave it. Only death can set me free" (Hamilton, 1942, p. 88). And, so it was, Narcissus pined away at the pool, fixed in his gaze. It is said that as his spirit crossed the river into the world of the dead, it leaned over the edge of the boat for one last look at itself reflected in the water. When some nymphs came to bury his body, they could not find it. Where it had been there was a beautiful new flower in full bloom. They called it Narcissus.

This is the curse which Nemesis carried out — "May he who loves not others love himself" (Hamilton, 1942, p. 88).

8. Perverse Expression of Sexuality

In the previous four chapters I have explored the ways of deadening sexuality. The methods discussed were those of lowering sexual arousal, clouding sexual awareness, retroflecting sexual action, and retroflecting sexual interaction. In each case there is the possibility of total deadening or of some degree of partial deadening. These can be termed "blocks" and "inhibitions" in the SCWC, respectively. The material from those four chapters is summarized in Figure 8.

Not only can sexuality be deadened, but it can be perverted. In my discussion of deadened sexuality I was dealing with sexuality which is dysfunctional to some degree because of psychological reasons. I now turn attention to a second realm where there is no sexual dysfunction, but where the sexual practice is sufficiently different from the norm to call attention. This distinction is also drawn by Helen Singer Kaplan (1974, p. 249): "Sexual disorders may be separated into the 'variations' and the 'dysfunctions.' The sexual variations, which are also called deviations and perversions, are characterized by good and pleasurable sexual functioning.

Figure 8. What, Where, How, and Why of Sexual Dysfunctions

Manifest Problem	Locus of Self-Interruption	Primary Mechanism of Self-Interruption	Toxic Script
(What?)	(Where?)	(How?)	(Why?)
Low sexual interest	Withdrawal → Want	Clouding of Awareness	Don't have sexual needs!
Low sexual excitement (erective impotence, non-lubrication)	Want → Arousal	Quieting of Arousal	Don't get sexually excited!
Lack of loving or lustful feelings	Arousal → Emotion	Clouding of Awareness	Don't feel love; don't feel lust!
Lack of sexual movement	Emotion → Action	Retroflection of Action	Don't act (sexually)!
Lack of sexual interaction	Action → Interaction	Retroflection of Interaction	Don't be sexual with any-one! (or some specific case of person)
Lack of enjoyment or ful-fillment, weakness or lack of orgasm	Interaction → Satisfaction	Clouding of Awareness	Don't enjoy sex!
Insatiability, or convert-ing satisfaction into aver-sion	Satisfaction → Withdrawal	Clouding of Awareness	Don't let go, you may not get another chance!

However, the sexual aim and/or object deviate from the norm. Men who practice variant forms of sexuality may have excellent erections and enjoyable, controlled ejaculations. Or the woman who is sexually deviant may be easily aroused, lubricate and be multiple orgastic. However, the deviant person is aroused by stimuli which are simply not exciting to most persons in our society. . . ."

The key to understanding the meaning of sexual perversion is contained in a short statement made by Kaplan in the above quotation, namely, "the sexual aim and/or object deviate from the norm." This statement derives from basic psychoanalytic theory. In a 1915 essay titled "Instincts and Their Vicissitudes," Freud (Rieff, 1963) delineated the parameters of an instinct. An instinct, being a "borderline concept between the mental and the physical (Rieff, 1963, p. 87)" has an impetus, an aim, an object, and a source. The *impetus* of an instinct is the motor element, or the force or energy which it represents. The *aim* of an instinct is satisfaction. There may be different paths to the goal of satisfaction, and therefore an instinct may have intermediate aims which may combine or be interchanged, leading to final satisfaction. The *object* of an instinct is that through which satisfaction can be obtained. The object, Freud instructs us, is the most variable parameter of the instinct. Objects become attached to the instinct only as a consequence of being discovered to be suitable for partial or total satisfaction. And, finally, the *source* of an instinct is the somatic process from which a stimulus arises, represented in mental life by the instinct.

The source and the impetus of the sexual urge are merely contextual in the consideration of perversion of that urge. Otherwise stated, the perversion of sexuality does not pertain either to the source of the urge or the strength of that urge. Perversion of sexuality refers to a change in aim or in object, as I called attention to in Kaplan's statement above.

Again, I find Freud to have some interesting things to say about sexual perversion. In his 1905 "Three Essays on the Theory of Sexuality" (Rothgeb, 1973), he clearly distinguished two types of sexual aberrations, those involving a deviation with respect to sexual object and those involving a deviation with respect to sexual aim. Under the rubric of deviations of sexual object, Freud discussed "inversion" (an obsolete term for male homosexuality) and the use of sexually immature persons and animals. As deviations of sexual aim Freud focused on "anatomical extensions" and on "fixations of preliminary sexual aims." These two terms lack the quality of being self-explanatory and so I will elaborate on them.

By "anatomical extensions" is meant sexual activity which in an anatomical sense extends beyond the regions of the body which are designed for sexual union. In other words, "anatomical extension" refers to "having sex" with parts not genital. For instance, oral-genital and oral-anal contact are, in the Freudian context, perversions of the normal sexual aim. Fetishes are related here, in that they are either nonsexual parts of a person, most often hair or feet, or are inanimate objects such as clothes, footwear, or articles of adornment. Again, these are unsuitable substitutes for the genitals with respect to satisfaction of the sexual urge.

In the phrase "fixation of preliminary sexual aims" the emphasis is on the undue prolongation of foreplay, to the point that it is the foreplay which is the goal. If foreplay is the preferred goal, the sexual aim has been diverted from that which offers most complete satisfaction, and, hence, is a perversion.

Freud (Rothgeb, 1973) emphasized that the pathological character of a perversion of sexual aim does not lie in the content of the new aim *per se*, but in its relationship to the norm. In other words, it is only when the perversion of sexual aim supplements genital-genital intercourse, when it becomes preferred and approaches exclusivity that it is clearly pathological. When the perversion of aim appears alongside the normal sexual aim, it can be of value inasmuch as it enhances the goal of satisfaction through genital-genital intercourse.

Following from the above, we can come to the classical psychoanalytic definition of sexual perversion: "Any form of adult sexual behaviour in which heterosexual intercourse is not the preferred goal" (Rycroft, 1968, p. 116). In Figure 9 I have outlined the Freudian view of sexual perversion.

At this point I feel the need to move to a metalevel of discourse. I have been writing about perversion, but now I want to move to a different level and comment on the process of writing about perversion. The problem is that to write about sex without moral and political bias is very difficult, perhaps impossible. Keleman (1982, p. xiii) acknowledged this: " . . . sexuality is now so political that one can barely make a statement about sex and love without

Figure 9. Freud's View of Sexual Perversion

The normal sexual instinct has a *source* (an endosomatic stimulation), an *impetus* (a force or degree of energy), an *object* (a heterosexual partner), and an *aim* (genital-genital intercourse leading to satisfaction through total reduction of sexual tension). In sexual perversion the object and/or the aim is diverted from that norm just stated.

Aberration of Object	*Aberration of Aim*
Inversion	Anatomical Extensions
Pedophilia	oral-genital
Bestiality	oral-anal
	fetish (body part)
	fetish (clothing)
	etc.
	Fixation of Preliminary
	Sexual Aims

being labeled a sexist, religious fanatic, an anti-lifer, or other epithets." My purpose here is not to proselytize for or against perversion, *per se*. Rather, I want to explore some of the psychological aspects of these variations from the format of sexuality which is designed for procreation. I want to describe and offer some degree of psychological understanding of sexual perversions.

I have chosen to use the word "perversion" because it is descriptively more complete than "variation" and has an historical place in the psychological literature. I emphasize that I use the term "perversion" in its technical and descriptive sense. The sexual behaviors discussed in the present chapter are perversions in the sense that they are preferred deviations from the paradigm of procreative sex. (Keep in mind that the paradigm of procreative sex is not limited in use to procreation.)

Of the two general categories of sexual perversion, aberration of object and aberration of aim, it is the former which has aroused the greater religious, moral and political indignation and protest. Just consider the intensity of negative sanction taken by both church and state toward homosexuality and pedophilia. In the case of bestiality there has been strong protest, but public knowledge of occurrences has been relatively small. Even though these are three subcategories of "aberration of object," they are so profoundly different one from another as to deserve an underscoring of this fact. One is a case of consenting adults. One is a case of an adult with a sexually or emotionally immature person. The third is a case of a person and an animal. Surely these must be considered quite independently for psychological understanding, let alone for moral and political/legal handling.

Perhaps the "aberrations of aim" have received less harsh treatment because of their occurrence in the presence of a penis and a vagina, even if it is not a penis-in-vagina scenario. In other words, the aberrations in aim are, in general, the taking of an aspect of love-making and making that aspect the primary focus or end in itself. As such, these perversions may in many cases not be so easy to recognize. Furthermore, in a sex negative culture or subculture the "fixation of preliminary sexual aims" may be encouraged and praised. Where sex is considered bad, less than "going all the way" is considered better. And so, foreplay as an end in itself may well be the perversion of choice in a sex negative society.

One more point that I want to make before returning to my psychological exploration of the perversions is that I will be excluding homosexuality. My reason is two-fold. First, this is in itself a topic with an enormous literature and is beyond the scope of what I feel expert enough to write about. Secondly, I believe that the topic is so obfuscated by moral, religious, and political/legal polemic that a relatively pure theoretical discussion on a psychological level is nearly impossible. Henceforth, my use of the term "perversion" does not include homosexuality.

I believe that Freud's theoretical work on perversion was very insightful. It has served as the basis for our understanding and has been used by many writers who have elaborated upon the basic theory. Kaplan (1974), whom I quoted a few paragraphs back, and Clifford Allen (1961), who wrote the entry on sexual perversions for the classic edited by Albert Ellis and Albert Abarbanel titled *The Encyclopedia of Sexual Behavior*, are but two notable examples. This is in addition to the considerable psychoanalytic literature on perversion since Freud's writing.

I want to elaborate on Freud's theory of perversion by relating it to the SCWC. (I have referred in the present chapter only to some aspects of Freud's theory of perversion. I have not presented his views on etiology, and leave it to the interested reader to follow up the references I have given.) By juxtaposing Freud's theory with the SCWC we get an expanded perspective, a more fine-grain analysis. We also add the dynamics of the SCWC discussed in earlier chapters (e.g. the feedback loops).

The Want of the SCWC pertains to the "source" of the sexual urge in Freud's theory. More specifically, it is the Need aspect of the Want which corresponds to the "source" (recall that the Want includes both Need and Preference). In the SCWC the Arousal → Emotion stages correspond to Freud's "impetus." Whereas he used a unitary concept, in the SCWC the phenomenon is acknowledged as two distinguishable phenomena, namely organismic Arousal and the differentiation of that excitement into a specific experience of Emotion. The experiencing of love, the lust, or the blending of the two may enhance the Arousal by means of a feedback loop.

Two of the stages of the SCWC pertain to the "aim" in Freud's theory, these being Action and Satisfaction. When discussing the "aim" of the instinct Freud saw the satisfaction which comes from reduction of the tension of the urge as the ultimate goal. However, prior to and in the service of the ultimate goal of satisfaction is the intermediate goal, or the activity which can lead to that ultimate goal. There is a degree of clarity added, I believe, by using the two terms "Action" and "Satisfaction" rather than the single term "aim" and to require that single term to carry two levels of meaning. This is particularly true in that it is only the intermediate goal which can be perverted, not the ultimate goal of satisfaction. In other words, it is not Satisfaction which can be perverted, it is Action, or the "means whereby."

The stage of Interaction in the SCWC corresponds to the "object" in Freud's formulation. A difference is that Freud was emphasizing the identity of the "object" while my emphasis has been on the inter-*action* with the person.

From this juxtaposition of the SCWC and Freud's theory of sexual perversion it becomes apparent that perversion has to do with the Action → Interaction sequence. That is, it is the Expression portion of the Contact Episode which is the locus of perversions of

Figure 10. A Relationship Between Freud's Instinct Theory
and the Sexual Contact/Withdrawal Cycle

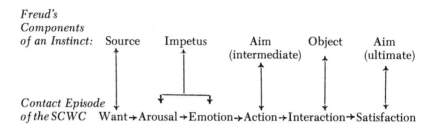

sexuality. As Allen (1961, p. 803) stated, consistent with what I have just noted about the SCWC, "It is mainly in the mode of expression and the nature of the sexual object that something goes wrong in the sexual pervert: either he behaves wrongly to the right object, or he chooses the wrong object." Freud's theory and the SCWC are related in Figure 10.

But, as we have seen earlier, each stage of the SCWC can affect previous stages through feedback loops. So, if the Action stage, the Interaction stage, or the entire Action → Interaction Sequence is perverted, what are the implications for the Awareness portion of the Contact Episode? First, the Want will change. The Need aspect of the Want, of course, is not affected. The Preference, however, is altered to become congruent with the perverted Action → Interaction Sequence. What this means is that there will be a shift in Awareness. The person will come to Want (a Preference) the form of sexuality which has been learned through the perverted activity. Therefore, I think it is accurate to speak of perverted sexual Wants, or more specifically of perverted sexual Preferences.

Once the perverted Preference is established, it is this which serves as a guide through the proceeding steps of the SCWC. Arousal, which is contributed to both by internal (endosomatic) and external stimulation, will be influenced by environmental stimuli which are congruent with the perverted Preference.

The stage of Emotion, too, can be affected. The blend of love and lust will tend to be altered toward an affect consistent with the Action → Interaction sequence forthcoming. In the case of sadistic Interaction, the emotion of hate will be blended with lust, and possibly, love.

The core of perverse sexuality, then, is the Action→Interaction sequence. Through feedback loops, the Want (Preference), the Arousal, and the Emotion will all be influenced. So, even though perversion is primarily an aberration within the Expression half of the SCWC, it reverberates in the Awareness half. Because of its pervasiveness, I think it is appropriate to speak of a perverted SCWC. Since the core of the perversion can be the Action, the Interaction, or both, I suggest the follow terms: Action-Perverted SCWC, Interaction-Perverted SCWC, and Action/Interaction-Perverted SCWC. I present these three forms of perverted SCWCs in Figure 11.

I want to derive a definition of perversion in the context of the SCWC. In this derivation I will share my sequence of thoughts. Adult sexuality has two basic purposes — procreation and pleasure. If the value is placed on procreation, then a particular sexual activity can be evaluated in terms of its efficacy. In other words, if a particular activity maximizes the probability of a conception, then it is good, not in a moral sense, but in a pragmatic sense. In terms of efficacy, with the value on procreation, penis-in-vagina intercourse to ejaculation is so clearly the best as to be a truism. Specific positions for intercourse, too, can be ranked as to how good they are in maximizing the probability of conception. In this context those positions which minimize the probability of conception, and activity other than that which allows conception would be perverse.

This view of sexuality is very narrow, and most educated people recognize that a much wider view of the value of sexuality is in order. In this wider valuing of sexuality pleasure is seen as of as much importance as procreation. Pleasure, in a broad sense, is the value of sexuality for all those people who want to be sexual and do not want to beget children.

In deriving a definition of perversion in the context of the SCWC I will use pleasure as the value base. Or, in keeping with my discussion in Chapter 1, the value is on sexual aliveness. That means that sex would be done in a manner which would provide the most experience of aliveness or pleasure, and with a partner who would allow for the most experience of aliveness or pleasure. The parts of the anatomy designed to give the greatest pleasure are, of course, the genitals. As I have discussed earlier in the book, there is a

Figure 11. The Perversions of the Sexual Contact/Withdrawal Cycle

Action-Perverted Contact Episode:

Want (perverted Preference) ⟶ Arousal (perverted stimuli) ⟶ Emotion (perverted affect) ⟶ Perverse Action ⟶ Interaction

Interaction-Perverted Contact Episode:

Want (perverted Preference) ⟶ Arousal (perverted stimuli) ⟶ Emotion (perverted affect) ⟶ Action ⟶ Perverse Interaction

Action/Interaction-Perverted Contact Episode:

Want (perverted Preference) ⟶ Arousal (perverted stimuli) ⟶ Emotion (perverted affect) ⟶ Perverse Action ⟶ Perverse Interaction paradigmatic action which is designed to provide the greatest focus on genital/body pleasure, that is, the thrusting of the pelvis. So, pelvic thrusting which presents the genitals for pleasurable contact is the paradigm Contact of genital sexuality. Implied in this is that the contact point would be one which would allow pleasure. In terms of Interaction, the choice would be judged in terms of whether or not the chosen is able to maximize satisfaction. In Chapter 1, in my discussion of masturbation, I pointed out that sex with oneself does not allow for the synergistic building of erotic energy which can occur in the case of sex with another. The meaning of love, closeness, sharing, and intimacy is greatest when the sex partner is in important ways one's peer. As one chooses partners further from peership, there is a commensurate lessening of the potential fullness of shared sexual experience. Another way of saying this is that sexual experience is diminished, relative to potential fullness, as mutuality is lost.

A further factor for consideration in terms of mutuality is whether the sexual activity which brings pleasure to one of the partners brings pleasure to the other, or conversely, is painful or harmful. Again, it is my contention that the greatest pleasure and meaning comes with mutuality in sexuality.

It follows, then, that the more removed one's sexuality is from those paradigms which maximize sexual pleasure, aliveness, and meaning, the more they have missed the mark. Otherwise stated, the more removed from those paradigms, the more perverted is the sexuality.

Those perversions which cause harm to others seem negative only, lacking in any civilized value. An example is the sexual abuse of children. Another is the beating of one's sex partner. Other perversions are relatively benign and the issue is only that of the effects on the one perpetrating the perversion. Examples of this would be sex with animals, and fetishes.

Perversion implies a preference for the activity, choosing it above more paradigmatic sexual activity when the choice is available. For some, the activity is not merely a preference, but the exclusive activity whereby that person can function sexually.

Thus, my definition of sexual perversion: *Perversion refers to a Sexual Contact/Withdrawal Cycle in which the chronically preferred or exclusive Action, Interaction, or both are different from*

those which maximize sexual pleasure and aliveness. This definition, by virtue of the phrase "chronically preferred or exclusive,"
allows that some activities may be practiced on occasion for con-
venience or for the sake of variety without their being perverted.
This pertains, of course, only to the benign activities. In addition,
the phrase implies that some of the benign activities may be practiced as preludes or adjuncts to paradigmatic genital sexuality.

A question which arises from this definition concerns the state
of Satisfaction in the SCWC. Remember, the perversion of the
Action → Interaction Sequence leads to an alteration in the
Awareness portion of the SCWC (see Figure 11). With respect to the
perverted Want (Preference) there may be Satisfaction. But,
relative to the normal Want, there will be a lack of complete
Satisfaction. The degree of this lack will correspond to the degree
of removal of the perverted Action → Interaction sequence from the
paradigmatic one. To illustrate by means of an extreme example,
no matter how much one enjoys fondling undergarments, and even
if one reaches orgasm in so doing, the Satisfaction which can be experienced through that cannot bring the richness and meaning
possible through sexual intercourse with one's peers.

Since it is the genitals which hold the potential for the greatest
sexual pleasure, the more one gets away from using one's genitals,
as a preference, the more that sexuality is perverted. This view is
in keeping with the psychoanalytic theory of psychosexual stages of
development. In its most simplified form, that theory states that in
the course of normal human development one evolves through
stages, and in each stage there is a zone of the body which is the
primary source of bodily pleasure. The erogenous zones included in
classical psychoanalysis are the oral, anal, and genital. Interestingly,
Elsworth Baker (1967) has suggested a fourth, the ocular. He
reports (1967, p. xii), "As far as I know no one has specifically done
this before, although Reich emphasized the importance of
armoring in the eye segment." So, if we add the ocular, we have
four major erogenous zones, the eyes, mouth, anus, and genitals,
in that order of primacy in normal development.

In psychoanalytic theory, then, if one of the pregenital
erogenous zones is preferred, this is evidence either of an arrest in
normal development (a fixation) or a return to an earlier stage of
development (a regression). So, we might think in terms of sexual

perversions as involving developmental fixations or regressions. The issue, again, is whether the eyes (looking), the mouth (kissing, sucking), and the anus (anal stimulation) are used for the sexual preliminaries, as adjuncts, and for variety, or are they used as a preferred or exclusive zone of pleasure, with the genitals de-emphasized or omitted.

Another point which I want to make is that the degree of perversion can be thought of in terms of which pregenital erogenous zone is preferred. Since they are arranged developmentally, and also in order of anatomical distance from the genitals, we can think of anal eroticism as one step away from the genitals, oral eroticism as two steps away and ocular eroticism as three steps away. This is also consistent with what might be commonly regarded as levels of sexual intimacy. Consider the intimacy involved with each stage—looking at the partner, kissing the partner, making contact with one's anus, and making contact with one's genitals.

Sometimes in a pairing, one of the sexual partners is more genitally primal than the other. For example, a man and a woman may partake of cunnilingus, exclusively. In this situation the woman is genitally involved whereas the man's involvement is two steps removed from his genitals. The intensity of pleasure available in this to the woman potentially far exceeds that available to the man. Also, she is the one more likely to lose control through orgasm, while he maintains control, relatively speaking. In this example, assuming that exclusive cunnilingus is a mutual choice, the degree of perversion is greater for the man than for the woman. He excludes his genitals, whereas she only excludes the special experience of genital-genital contact, and with that the opportunity for mutual orgasm.

Consider the following sexual activities of a man and woman. In each case there is a particular potential for sexual pleasure. A similar list of sexual activities could be construed for a man-man pairing or a woman-woman pairing.

Given that there are two potentially active people involved, some combinations of these activities can be engaged in simultaneously. There is also the possibility of the introduction of sexual paraphernalia. These devices can be viewed as mechanical substitutes for the penis or vagina. And so we see the possibility of great variety of sexual Action, providing the excitement of novelty, ample foreplay, or perversion.

Man	Woman
Penis	Vagina (clitoris)
Penis	Anus
Penis	Mouth
Penis	Hand
Penis	Skin surface (between breasts, etc.)
Anus	Mouth
Anus	Hand
Mouth	Vagina (clitoris)
Mouth	Anus
Mouth	Mouth
Mouth	Skin surface (breasts, neck, etc.)
Hand	Vagina (clitoris)
Hand	Anus
Hand	Skin surface (breasts, etc.)
Skin surface	Mouth
Skin surface	Hand
Skin surface	Skin surface

Now that I have defined a perverted SCWC, one implication is that there can be sexual deadening and sexual perversion cooperating. That is to say, the perverted SCWC has the same stages and dynamics as a natural SCWC, and is therefore also susceptible to the methods of deadening which have been explored in previous chapters. This means that there are various possible levels of aliveness or levels of functioning within the context of a particular perversion. Boldness versus inhibition is just as much an issue in the realm of perverted sexuality as it is in natural sexuality. When there is a block, thus preventing overt expression of the perverted sexuality, the term "latent" may be in order. Thus, one may speak of a "latent fetishist," a "latent voyeur," a "latent exhibitionist," and so forth.

The interesting twist in the case of an inhibition or a block in a perverted SCWC is that oftentimes the introject which is operating is not a toxic voice which forbids sexual aliveness. Rather, it is a voice which represents a position of decent, respectful treatment of one's self and others. Consider, for example, the case of a latent pedophile who is blocked by an introjected voice which says, in essence, "You should not be sexual with children because it could seriously harm them." The perverted Preference may be strong, but the introjected message may be sufficient to lead to a self-interruption in that perverted SCWC.

Following the definition of perversion in the context of the SCWC, which I offered above, various classical perversions can be arranged in terms of whether they involve a perversion of Action, perversion of Interaction, or both. I present this in summary in Figure 12. My major sources for lists of classical perversions and their definitions are Allen (1961) and Karpman (1962). I have presented this material in matrix form to suggest the possible perverse Action/Interaction combinations. I leave it to the reader to think of examples of each of these. All of the combinations are possible, although many of them are extremely rare.

There are two more perversions which are of sufficient prominence to deserve mention, but which I have not explicitly included in Figure 12. They are, however, implicitly present, as I shall show. First is pornography, or the preference for sexually explicit pictures and writing. The subject matter may include natural sexuality, but a large proportion of pornographic material involves the various perversions. As a perversion, pornography is closely akin to scoptophilia, but is even another step removed from actual participation with the other person or persons. The person whose preference is for pornography has only a media representation of sexual material — a picture, a film, an audio tape, a written story. These media representations guarantee that no person to person contact will be made, so the viewer is very safe.

The second perversion which is only implicit in Figure 12 is transvestism, or the wearing of clothes of the opposite sex for sexual purposes. I think that transvestism can accurately be thought of as a special case of fetishism. Stoller (1968, p. 176) has defined adult male transvestism as " . . . completely pleasurable; it is fetishistic, intermittent cross-dressing in a biological normal man who does not question that he is male. . . . " (Stoller points out that there is another type of transvestism in which the man desires for periods of time to pass as a woman. For him, the desire is to be a "phallic woman." This second type represents a much more complex dynamic than simply that of a fetishist. Stoller maintains that there

Figure 12. Action Perversions, Interaction Perversions, and Combined Action/Interaction Perversions

Action:	Interactions: Autosexuality (self)	Bestiality (Zooerasty) (animal)	Gerontosexuality (elderly person)	Infanto-sexuality (Pedophilia) (Carnal abuse) (child)	Necrophilia (cadaver)
Analism (Buggery)				(Pederasty)	
Coprophilia (love of excrement)					
Exhibitionism (Indecent exposure)					
Fetishism (major - body parts, minor - objects)					
Frottage (rubbing against people)		(Zoophilia)			
Oralism					
Sadomasochism					(Necrosadism) (Vampirism)
Scoptophilia (Voyeurism)					

are no true female transvestites. That is, he claims that he has never seen a woman who was an "intermittent, fetishistic cross-dresser." There are, of course, women who dress as men and live as men but for those women who pass as men [female transsexuals] the men's clothing has no erotic value. Also, there are culturally supported "transvestic" tendencies wherein clothing styles may allow or even dictate masculinization in women's dress. Again, in this case the clothing does not have erotic value for the wearer.)

Unlike the deadening of sexuality, as explored in earlier chapters, the perversions are ways of keeping sexuality alive. They are, in a sense, alternate routes. In some cases these alternate routes evoke the disdain of those who do not share in them. In other cases, these alternate routes are simply of such a nature that they offer far less richness and meaning than the more conventional route.

The vast variety of sexual behaviors in which human beings engage bespeaks both an impressive creativity and the strength of the sexual urge. The perversions attest to what can become of a sexual urge which is not allowed a natural course of expression. Turning once again to the SCWC, a distinction becomes clear between perversion and dysfunction of the Action → Interaction sequence. With a simple inhibition or block of Action or Interaction the SCWC is weak or incomplete, respectively. As I discussed in Chapter 3, the energy of the sexual urge in a blocked or inhibited SCWC does not just go away, but must be dealt with organismically. This, as I explained, can lead to symptoms — psychological, physiological, or both, and even to dramatic disease processes. But with some forms of perverse SCWCs, assuming that there is not also a self-interruption, the sexual energy does get processed.

So, to state this again, in a somewhat different way, sexual psychopathology involves two subcategories: sexual dysfunction and sexual perversion. In both cases there is a pattern of habitual self-interruption in the Sexual Contact/Withdrawal Cycle. But in the case of perversion, there is a shift from the natural SCWC to a perverted SCWC. If in the perverted SCWC there is an inhibition or a block that leaves unprocessed energy and the same sequela as in the self-interrupted natural SCWC.

The intriguing question is why would one person simply self-interrupt a SCWC at the point of Action or Interaction and another person would self-interrupt and substitute a perverted Action or Interaction, thus establishing a perverted SCWC? A partial answer lies once again with the toxic introject. Whereas, as summarized in Figure 8, the toxic script is essentially "Don't act (sexually)" or "Don't be sexual with anyone!" (or some specific class of person) in the case of a simple self-interruption, in the case of perversion there is a twist. The twist is that the toxic script is not all-inclusive, but is taken to prohibit the natural Action-Interaction sequence, but not some perverse one. In fact, in some instances the toxic script gives explicit permission for the perverted SCWC. An example is the mother who encourages her son to wear his sister's underwear.

The focus of perversion, as already shown, is on the Action → Interaction sequence, and this forms the basis for the classification schema of Figure 12. I want now to relate the perversion of Action to some aspects of Reichian theory. Remember, the primary pathological mechanism for the inhibition or block of Action is retroflection. In Chapter 6 I showed that retroflection of Action is equivalent to Reich's concept of "body armor." So, we can say that retroflection of sexual Action, or pelvic armoring, is an aspect of the path to perverted sexual Action. The idea is that the primary sexual impulse, when blocked or severely inhibited, can be converted into a secondary sexual impulse, or perversion. Reich (1973, p. 294) stated clearly, "The inhibition of the primary impulse produces a secondary impulse. . . ." This view is nicely elaborated by Baker (1967, p. xxiv), "Natural strivings, when they pass through armor, change from soft to harsh." Consider the Action perversions in Figure 12, with respect to their being "secondary impulses." In terms of harshness, sadomasochism stands out as the most obvious example.

So, we see that sex is highly diverse in its manifestations. When prevented from following its natural path, it can move into other realms, some even exotic. But, in the extreme, these alternate paths are psychologically and physically harmful to perpetrator and partner, alike. Sometimes the manifest sexuality is only symbolic of the full, natural expression. Whatever the toxic introject, the sexual urge presses for some expression, be it inhibited, fragmentary, symbolic, or distorted. Perhaps, now, the statement of Aldous Huxley in *Eyeless in Gaza* has more meaning, "Chastity — the most unnatural of the sexual perversions."

9. Sexual Life, Sexual Morals, and Sexual Politics

In this, the final chapter, I want to delve into some aspects of the philosophical context of sexual aliveness. Thus far, I have explored the meaning of sexual aliveness, the natural rhythms of sex, the disruptions of the natural rhythms, with the specific organismic mechanisms for disruption, and the perverse expression of sex. My bias, throughout, has been sexual aliveness as a value. And, now, what of the politics and the morals of sexual aliveness?

Sexuality is always expressed within some cultural context, and therefore always within the context of a political/moral system. Even the discussion of sexuality cannot escape such context. As stated by Szasz (1980, p. 152), "Since human sexual behavior is culturally shaped, anyone who writes about it must do so from a particular ethical and political perspective." Because this is so, much clarity is gained by recognizing as much as possible, and in relative terms, the level of discourse on sexuality. In other words, *it is helpful to distinguish about sexuality what is biological, what is psychological, what is sociological, what is political, and what is moral.* There has been much confusion perpetrated by the failure to acknowledge these distinctions. Just one example is the warning by the sex reformers (Strong, 1983, p. 138), "*Any* girl who will give herself to you has probably given herself to others who have diseased her." Clearly, the position taken is a moral position, but is stated as if it were a statement concerning medical (biological) knowledge. This warning is designed to influence behavior, to discourage sex outside marriage. It confuses "illicit" relations with prostitution and uses implied medical knowledge to make a moral point. Such confusions abound in the writings on sexuality.

Sexuality is based in our psychobiology and lived out in a cultural context wherein the natural sexual urge is filtered. The result is sexual repression, sexual distortion, or the natural expression of sexuality in all of its myriad forms.

There have been several cultural movements which have profoundly affected sexual attitudes and behaviors in the United States. These include Catholicism, Puritanism, the prevailing attitudes of the Victorian era, and the sexology movement. These movements represent four of the major threads which intertwine throughout the fabric of American sexuality. I want to explore each of these in relation to the value of sexual aliveness.

Catholicism places high value on celibacy. Not only does Catholicism emphasize the Virgin Mary more than does any Protestant sect of Christianity, but it requires its priests to vow celibacy. As "Brides of Christ," women who enter the holy orders are, too, required to be celibate. For those to whom the priests and nuns minister, there are strict rules for being sexual. Basically, sex outside marriage is seen as sinful. Sex is for procreation. Hence, birth control is a sin, abortion is a sin, premarital sex is a sin, extramarital sex is a sin, and masturbation is a sin. In addition, divorce is not allowed. Obviously, the Catholic position on sexuality is extremely conservative, and, I believe it is safe to say, basically sex-negative.

The Puritan view on sexuality is commonly misunderstood. The Puritan position is a conservative one, to be sure, but it acknowledges sexuality as a part of human nature, a part to be enjoyed. One minister expressed in writing his horror at " . . . that Popish conceit of the Excellency of Virginity" (Morgan, 1983, p. 6). The Puritans were impressed with the view that the Holy Spirit has said, "It is not good that man should be alone." So, sexual intercourse was seen as a necessity, but marriage the only proper context for it. The only limitation which Puritanism placed on sex within marriage was that sex must not interfere with religion. Morgan (1983) tells us that the early Puritans were far from ascetics, and that they asked only that the pleasures of the flesh be subordinated to the pursuit of the glory of God.

The Puritans did take a hostile stand toward sex outside marriage, and passed laws to punish adultery with death, and fornication with whipping. Morgan (1983) presents evidence, however, that sexual offenses were commonplace, and the harsh laws were rarely enforced. Rather than emphasize punishment for sexual offenses, the Puritans worked toward prevention by encouraging early marriage. Marriage was seen as the way to discourage fornication, and successful marriage as the way to discourage adultery. Much of the legal intervention by the Puritans was in an effort to "enforce" successful marriage. With Puritanism, then, we see permission for active sexuality within marriage, with strong prohibitions against any form of sexuality outside marriage. In addition, there is serious interference with personal liberty by virtue of the attempted legal enforcement of the ideal. This is a position of highly restricted sexuality.

The attitudes of the Victorians differ from Catholicism and Puritanism in that they are not religiously based. They are a set of secular ideas which contain some very definite views about sexuality. Male sexuality and female sexuality are regarded quite differently, and when these views are combined there emerges a clear statement of Victorian sexuality. The following is a necessarily oversimplified summary of the Victorian view of woman.

Throughout history, from ancient Greece to modern Western civilization, women had generally been thought to desire and enjoy sex more than men. The Victorians took a radically opposite view, making it a central tenet that women lack sexual passion. "Passionlessness" is the basis of Victorian female sexual ideology (Cott, 1983). This doctrine of passionlessness was tied to the rise of evangelical religion between the late 1700s and the early 1800s (Cott, 1983). Female chastity came to be seen as the archetype for human morality. Conversely, sex was seen as the basest of human tendencies, the aberrations of which were punished through disease and mental anguish. Whatever stimulated erotic emotions in a young girl would cause a corresponding development of her sex organs, "excessive excitement," and, in turn, disease (Haller, 1983). So, girls were advised to play a passive role with men, and to express not the slightest evidence of reciprocating love until the man declared intention of matrimony.

In marriage, sex was only for procreation, and to be endured to that end. Not only was pleasure for the woman not valued, but it was believed that "any spasmodic convulsion" on the part of the woman during intercourse would interfere with the conception (Haller, 1983). Birth control, of course, was strongly denounced. Sex during pregnancy was improper not only because it could not be of any good purpose (procreation), but was also believed to be damaging to the future character, morals, and physical appearance of the unborn child.

The Victorian view of male sexuality was built around the doctrine of the "spermatic economy." This view, central to the mainstream beliefs of the nineteenth century, was a revival of the medieval idea that men possess a limited reserve of sexual fluid. Use of sexual fluid for pleasure, or for overindulgence in procreative sex represented a waste, and as such, an evil (Barker-Benefield, 1983). A concupiscent woman, therefore, should be avoided, as she would be an evil "sperm absorber." But, perhaps the greatest evil to be avoided was masturbation. The discharge of sperm was believed to "obliterate," "prostrate," and "blot out" all of the "energies of the system." "Runts," feeble infants, and girls could result from debilitated sperm, old men's prostrated sperm, businessmen's tired sperm, masturbators' exhausted sperm, debauchers' exceeded sperm, contraceptors' impeded sperm, cowards' unpatriotic sperm, and newlyweds' green sperm (Barker-Benefield, 1983). Medical advice was available for keeping sperm at a healthy level. So, masturbation was seen as "pollution."

The Victorian view of sexuality can be summarized by the two concepts of passionlessness of women and the spermatic economy of men. The implication of these doctrines, when combined, is that sex is to be strictly reserved for procreation. Sex for pleasure is against the nature of woman, and is a dangerous, debilitating activity for man. The basis for such belief is not in religion, but in purported medical fact. The Victorian way is clearly sex-negative.

The final thread in the American sexual fabric is that of

sexology. Sexology is the scientific study of sex, and as such often purports to be "objective" and beyond sociopolitical bias. Rather than being based in religious ideology, it is based in scientific investigation of sexual phenomena. The first big boost to this movement was the early psychoanalytic work of Freud. The result was a view which was shocking to the staunch Victorians. The Victorian view was challenged by the new liberalism of the scientist and the early twentieth century novelist.

The major radical statement of the new movement was that pleasure, independent of conception, is as legitimate an end of sexual activity in marriage as is procreation (Strong, 1983). The next step in the sexology movement was the development of social science techniques in the early twentieth century which allowed statistical investigations of many aspects of sexuality. The major contribution of this second wave of sexology, I believe, was the legitimization of the investigation of things sexual. By the mid–1940s at least 19 investigations of human sexuality had been reported. And, then the blockbuster of 1948 hit, Alfred C. Kinsey's *Sexual Behavior in the Human Male*.

Kinsey's work was hailed as one of the most influential books of the twentieth century. Kinsey's name, a household word, became synonymous with liberal views of sex. George Gallup reported that fully 20 percent of all Americans had at least heard of Kinsey's report, if not read it (Moranty, 1983). The following emerged as major findings by Kinsey:

Male masturbation was almost universal.
Ninety-five percent of men established a regular sexual outlet by age fifteen.
Men reached peak sexual activity in their late teens.
Thirty-seven percent of American men had engaged in homosexual behavior involving orgasm.
Eighty-six percent of the men had had premarital intercourse.
Almost all men in the sample had engaged in premarital petting, much of it to the point of orgasm.
Half of the men had had extramarital intercourse.
There were no basic physiological differences between the sexual responses of men and women.
The lack of nerve endings in the interior vagina make it insensitive to the touch. (This implied that intercourse was not the most efficient method for a woman to achieve sexual pleasure.)

Sixty-two percent of the women masturbated.

Ninety percent of the women had engaged in premarital petting.

Fifty percent of the women had had premarital intercourse.

There was a steady rise in the number of women reaching orgasm in marital intercourse in the decades following World War I.

Precoital petting techniques in marriage had become more common and varied during this same period.

Lower- and working-class men reported a higher incidence of premarital intercourse, tended to view extended foreplay as "unnatural," were less likely to have sex in the nude, masturbated less frequently, and tended to see sex as an uncontrollable impulse.

Middle-class and college-educated men, in contrast, tended to be virgins at the time of marriage, tended to pet and masturbate more, and tended to view sex more moralistically.

Males who were upwardly or downwardly mobile tended to take on the sexual attitudes and behaviors of their destined class long before the shift in class was made.

From his findings Kinsey drew several interesting conclusions. Among these are the following:

Sexual adjustment is of central importance in stable unions.

Modern education conditions attitudes towards sex which interfere with successful sexual adjustment in marriage, e.g., requiring the delay of sexual expression until marriage creates a sexual maladjustment which may require years of marriage to overcome.

The variations of sexuality found bring into question our previous notions of what is right or wrong, normal or abnormal.

Reaching orgasm is a learned skill for women, and therefore takes time to learn.

Kinsey provided a quantified view of a large sampling of sexual behavior. This presentation of data was a statement of what Americans were doing sexually. But, Kinsey went beyond the descriptive level by suggesting that since certain sexual behaviors showed a degree of prevalence, they must have a basis in human biology, and therefore must be normal. In doing this, Kinsey was a major figure in the move towards the liberalization of sexual attitudes and sexual behaviors. His work also helped lay the foundation for the modern approaches to sex therapy.

So, even the work of a biological scientist such as Kinsey (he built his early career on his expertise on the gall wasp), can easily cross into the realm of the moral and the political. Another sexologist who made this crossover, and did so even more energetically, was Wilhelm Reich. I have drawn on much of Reich's work already in this book. His more political extrapolations are thoroughly worked out in *The Sexual Revolution*, first published in English in 1945 (Reich, 1969). Based on his clinical experience and his theories about sexuality, Reich developed his "sexpolitics," with a platform of sexual rights and freedoms (Mann and Hoffman, 1980). The main points are as follows:

1. An end to housing shortage which makes it difficult for young lovers to find privacy.

2. Abolition of all legal restraints on birth control, abortion, and homosexuality.

3. More liberal divorce laws.

4. Free availability and distribution of contraceptives to everyone (including adolescents).

5. Sex education through the mass media.

6. Sex counseling provided by virtually all business firms.

7. Abolition of any laws which prohibit sex education.

8. Conjugal rights for prisoners.

The basis for this platform was Reich's belief in sexual self-regulation and responsibility for everyone — children, adolescents, adults.

And, so, Freud, Reich, Kinsey, and others offered another thread into the fabric of American sexuality, a thread unwound from the spool of science, but one which fully entered the warp and the woof of a political-moral weave.

We now live in a culture which has been influenced by the Catholic, Puritan, and Victorian views of sex, on the conservative side, and by sexology, on the liberal side. There are additional influences, as well. But, it is these four, and their combinations, which I see most in evidence in my clinical experience. Interestingly, religious persuasion often seems not to be an adequate predictor of sexual attitudes. So, regardless of one's acclaimed religion, any combination of these four molders of sexual attitudes and behaviors may be found. Of course, whenever the sexology position is found in combination with one of the others, there is a situation of extreme cognitive dissonance.

The basic issue of sexual morality is which sexual behavior is right and which is wrong. The basic issue of sexual politics is to what extent the government intervenes to restrain or to encourage certain sexual behaviors.

Let us look at the moral issue first. My bias, as I have stated several times throughout this book, is for sexual aliveness. I see that which enlivens as good, that which deadens as bad. I resonate with Reich's belief in self-regulation and responsibility in sex. Self-regulation is respectful, respectful of one's organismic wisdom. Self-regulation means that one responds when a sexual urge grows strong, and also that one not force sex when one's sexual urge is not experienced. In other words, sexual behavior would be based in natural desire rather than in expectations of others.

Although a truism, I think it is worth stating that only I can experience myself. Only I have the vantage point from within. Therefore, I am in the best position of anyone to know when and what sexual expression is appropriate for me. Not only is the timing of my sexual expression best chosen by me, but the way I express sexually is also best guided by my own experiencing of pleasure and displeasure. If I allow myself an experimental attitude, I will discover whether or not a particular sexual activity is satisfying. I don't have to be told what feels good. I am the only expert on my own feelings and sensations. So, I believe that self-regulation is the process which best determines both the when and the how of one's sexuality. My awareness informs me.

Responsibility in sex refers to at least three areas. First is the responsibility towards the other person. This means to act in such a manner as to respect the welfare and feelings of one's sex partner, and not to exploit the other. Second is responsibility for consequences, or the willingness to deal with the outcome or repercussions of one's sexual behavior in a respectful manner. The third area of responsibility, as pointed out by Paul Goodman (1977) is responsibility to one's own feelings. This means to respond to the inner urge for sexual expression, and as such, brings us back to respect for one's self-regulative process in sex.

The popular moral position toward sex which is held by liberals is the doctrine of "consenting adults." This doctrine states that any sexual behavior that is engaged in by consenting adults, in a private setting, is acceptable. The term "consenting adults" implies, of course, that the participants have reached maturity and are able to decide what they want to do, in a responsible manner. This position seems to be a good guideline. It gives personal freedom and mutual responsibility to the participants.

Reich (1980) suggested that of all the bodily functions, the genital function is the one most susceptible to social interference. And, of all the bodily functions, it seems that the genital function has received more emotionally charged political action than any other. Political control is focused on both the self-regulation and the responsibility aspects of sexual morality. Interestingly, Reich (1980) viewed this political control of sex as resulting in part from the fact that morality is determined by socioeconomic interests.

Modern Western society was seen by Reich as basically sex-negative. That is, society is not pro-sex, it does not recognize and support healthy sex lives. This position is echoed in the Gestalt literature. For example, Perls, Hefferline, and Goodman (1951, p. 410) wrote, " . . . anti-sexual society is designed to produce this traumatic situation with maximum frequency and efficiency." The traumatic situation to which they were referring was fright, a common context for that being secretive sex.

The justification given for the use of political and even legal control of any aspect of sexuality is the belief that the sexual impulse, left uncontrolled from without, is dangerous. The belief is that the basic sexual urge is inevitably at variance with important social values. If there are not strict social and legal negative sanctions, the base, animal urges will manifest and erode society. This position seems to come from the Victorian point of view.

A specific target of the proponents of close legal control of sex is the area of work. Their belief is that sex, uncontrolled by an external source, would distract from productivity. I have heard a version of this belief time and time again from patients. Having this belief as an element of their toxic scripts, they force themselves to work hard, feel resentful about how hard they "have" to work, and usually become depressed. Their fear, which they often can articulate, is that if they ever stop forcing work, and allow pleasure, they will never work again. One patient expressed to me that if he took time off and just had fun, he would probably become a bum for the rest of his life. This shows a lack of faith in the rhythm which develops out of organismic self-regulation.

Reich (1980) addressed this issue of sexual satisfaction and its relation to work. He came to several interesting conclusions based on data from the Clinic for Work Disturbances. First, he concluded that *low social productivity increases sexual excitation*. This is based on the finding that working men who were out of work and spent long periods of time in inactivity experienced a great deal of sexual excitation. Second, *sexual satisfaction actually increases the ability to work*. Joy in work can be shown often to follow a satisfying sexual experience. This is understandable in that a satisfying sexual experience, moving one into the natural Withdrawal stage of the SCWC, leaves one free from sexual tension which would be pressing for satisfaction, and thus distracting one from the task at hand. In addition, consider the "glow," the sense of centeredness and well-being which follows satisfying sex. Reich offers the phenomenological observations that following a satisfying sexual experience there often is an increased self-confidence, a greater sense of purposefulness, and a sense of strength. It is an understanding of this which has led certain athletes, for instance, to arrange for a sexual encounter a few hours before their public performance.

Third, Reich concluded that *in the long run the ability to work is disturbed by unsatisfied sexuality*. The awareness of sexual tension can be avoided for some period of time, but this avoidance takes a great deal of energy. So if one throws herself or himself into long hours of hard work, sexuality may be avoided and on the surface what is manifest is great productivity. Such people are exhibiting what Reich (1980) termed the "rage to work." His clinical finding was that such people are afraid to rest because rest would not allow them to avoid sexual fantasies or the experiencing of their sexual urges. My own clinical experience is consistent with this. Eventually, though, the unsatisfied sexual urge cannot be contained, and the avoidance no longer works. It may take months or even years, but eventually the compensation breaks down and symptoms will appear which clearly interfere with work.

Reich clearly took the position that sexuality has a natural goodness. Rather than being basically bad and therefore needing to be controlled by law and restrictive social convention, sex is naturally good, but easily gets distorted into bad forms by the very laws and conventions designed to save us from it. Earlier I discussed the Reichian view of the development of harsh secondary drives when primary drives are not allowed natural expression. In *The Sexual Revolution* Reich (1969, p. 22) states this: "Moral regulation represses and keeps from gratification the *natural* biological needs. This results in *secondary, pathologically antisocial* impulses. These, in turn, have to be inhibited of necessity."

The distinction between natural biological needs and secondary, pathological antisocial impulses is emphasized strongly by Reich. His idea is far from the doctrine of "anything goes." But, as long as the natural impulse and the secondary impulses are not differentiated, as is the case in authoritarian societies, according to Reich, the suppression of the antisocial forms of sexuality will include the suppression of natural sexuality as well. So, moral regulation is *per se* sex-negative. It denies the natural sexual needs and fails to recognize the natural sex-economy which is reflected in the SCWC, as presented in the present book.

This view is echoed by Keleman (1982) when he writes that the frustration of natural sexual arousal leads to violent sex. Given that concupiscence is part of the human condition, a part of human "existentialia," it seems that the issue is how to facilitate sexual expression which is both personally satisfying and socially beneficial. This issue, I believe, is the appropriate focus of sex education. The major problem which stands in the way of such sex education is deeply embedded not only in our sociopolitical structure, but our personal psychology, as well.

The problem is insightfully presented by Reich (1973, p. 233) in the following passage.

> The patriarchal, authoritarian era of human history has attempted to hold the asocial impulses in check by means of compulsive moralistic prohibitions. It is in this way that civilized man ... developed a psychic structure consisting of three layers. On the surface, he wears an artificial mask of self-control, compulsive insincere politeness, and pseudo sociality. This mask conceals the second layer ... in which sadism, avarice, lasciviousness, envy, perversions of all kinds ... are held in check without, however, being deprived of the slightest amount of energy. This second layer is the artificial product of a sex-negating culture and is usually experienced consciously as a gaping inner emptiness and desolation. Beneath it, in the depth, natural sociality and sexuality, spontaneous joy in work,

the capacity for love, exist and operate. This third and deepest layer, which represents the biological core of the human structure, is unconscious, and it is feared. It is at a variance with every aspect of authoritarian education and control. At the same time, it is the only real hope man has of one day mastering social misery.

The call is for a sex-positive society, a society in which sexuality is valued for procreation and valued for pleasure. This means a society where only violent sex is legally dealt with, where sexual acts of force such as rape and child molestation are recognized as the only "illegal" forms of sex. Children would be allowed and supported in their natural curiosity and experimentation. Adults would offer guidance, education, and protection from exploitation. Consenting adults, themselves, would be given the freedom to experiment, learn, grow, and evolve in their own individual sexuality. This may be idealistic. I do know that we are a long way from such an activity.

In the past few years there have been some changes which have been labeled the "sexual revolution." I believe that to call the changes a revolution is somewhat misleading. There has been a "going public" with sensuality, to be sure. That is to say, in the past two decades there has been a dramatic increase in open, public stimulation of sexual arousal. From miniskirts and topless "go-go" dancing to "streaking" and X-rated films, and from wet T-shirt contests and adult book stores to *Playboy*, *Penthouse*, and sexually explicit popular music, there has been a huge industry in "turning America on" sexually. But, in presenting this trend as a revolution, it is implied that there is a new openness and acceptance of sexuality. What there is, is a massive movement of erotic stimulation. As all of this arousing material is offered through radio, television, newspapers, magazines, live performances, and clothing fashions, the message is "look, get excited, but don't touch!" This is so much the case that Keleman (1982) has asserted that as a society we are overaroused and sensorily inflated, and that overstimulation is a national crisis. The point that must be remembered is that arousal is not satisfaction.

The massive movement of erotic stimulation affects the Awareness half of the Contact Episode of the SCWC, primarily. My contention, based on my personal clinical experience and my observations in my social world, is that the change in American sexuality over the past two decades or so has been primarily an increase in public sexual arousal, and not in sexual Satisfaction through richly meaningful sexuality. In terms of the SCWC I am drawing attention to the current emphasis on the Awareness half to the neglect of the Expression half of Contact.

Lowen (1963) has drawn essentially the same distinction in his writing about the "sensualist" and the "sexualist." As he uses the terms, sensuality is aimed at increasing sexual excitement, whereas sexuality is oriented toward the satisfaction of orgastic discharge. The sensualist is one who, because of a lack of inner aliveness and fear of orgasm, is primarily interested in foreplay and stimulation. For her or him the search for sexual excitement becomes an end in itself. As I discussed in the previous chapter, the preference for foreplay as opposed to orgasm is a perversion of sexuality. Lowen uses the term "sexualist" for one who is oriented toward orgastic satisfaction and uses sensuality in support of that end. I find Lowen's conclusion consistent with the contention which I stated above. In his words (Lowen, 1963, p. 29), "It is my experience that our sexual sophistication has lowered the barriers to sensuality without significantly affecting or relieving orgasm-anxiety." So, I am saying the same thing, now, over twenty years later.

I want to tie what I have just written back into the above mention of Keleman's (1982) statement on violent sex. What Keleman said is that strong sexual arousal by insistent stimuli while one is unable to obtain satisfaction can cause a violent form of sexuality. It appears to me, consistent with what other writers have written, that there is a large industry devoted to insistent sexual stimulation, and, at the same time considerable inhibition of natural sexual expression. With many people blocked or inhibited in the Action → Interaction → Satisfaction sequence, and still widely exposed to insistent sexual stimulation, there can only result a common sexual frustration and violence of sexuality.

Violence results, I believe, when out of such sexual frustration the feeling of love is bypassed, leaving lust as the primary sexual emotion. In addition, the insistence of the sexual stimulation may press for sexual preferences which are artificial for the person, preferences which are not a natural development from the inner person. These "public preferences" may interfere with the development of one's personal preferences which require time and experimentation. The violence is not necessarily dramatic, as in rape or such. More often it is a subtle violence to oneself or one's partner, such as having sex when one does not desire it from within, or having sex to present an image.

Incidentally, I believe that it is this violent sex in its subtle forms which is being reacted against by the proponents of the so-called "new celibacy." The "new celibacy" appears to me to be an escape from sex based on public overstimulation. If the only alternatives seen are sex which involves overstimulation, frustration, and violence to the integrity of one's self or of one's partner, or no sex, then the latter may be an appealing alternative. But, both of those alternatives involve sexual deadening. The meaningful choice is neither of these but instead the choice of being sexually alive.

Unfortunately, sex education programs in the schools have probably done very little to relieve the situation of subtle violence in sex. The majority of such programs that I know about focus on reproductive biology, teaching children the basic anatomy and physiology of sex. Szasz (1980) has written that various reports on sex education programs in the public schools make it clear that these courses teach "a minimum of biological science" and a "maximum of an anti-interpersonal sexual ideology." Szasz has been highly critical of these programs in his demonstration of the degree of hidden moral and political dimensions of sex education throughout the grade school and the high school levels. What is missing, in my opinion, is the delving into the personal, psychological meaning of sex. I believe that this could be done in sex education programs.

Perhaps the urge to contact one's natural sexuality is reflected on the societal level by various cultural changes, both evolutionary and revolutionary. The forces for sexual freedom and for sexual control vie for dominance. And, it seems clear that as personal freedoms in general are legislated away, sexual freedoms are specifically targeted.

The ultimate freedom of the biological aspect of self surely is to be sexual. And, so I close this book with one wish for all: to thine own sexual self, be true.

References

Chapter 1

Adam, M. *Wandering in Eden*. New York: Alfred A. Knopf, 1976.

Bean, O. *Me and the Orgone*. New York: St. Martin's Press, 1971.

Ellis, A., and Abarbanel, A. (eds.) *The Encyclopedia of Sexual Behavior*. New York: Hawthorn, 1961.

Holroyd, S., and Holroyd, S. *Sexual Loving*. New York: Exeter Books, 1979.

Keleman, S. *In Defense of Heterosexuality*. Berkeley, Calif.: Center Press, 1982.

Lowen, A. *Sex and Personality*. New York: Institute of Bioenergetic Analysis, 1963.

_____. *Fear of Life*. New York: Collier, 1980.

Mann, W. *Orgone, Reich, and Eros*. New York: Touchstone, 1973.

Offit, A. *Night Thoughts: Reflections of a Sex Therapist*. New York: Congdon and Lattès, 1981.

Reich, W. *The Function of the Orgasm*. New York: Touchstone, 1973.

_____. *Listen, Little Man!* New York: Farrar, Straus and Giroux, 1974.

_____. *Genitality in the Theory and Therapy of Neurosis*. New York: Farrar, Straus and Giroux, 1980.

Smith, E. *The Body in Psychotherapy*. Jefferson, N.C.: McFarland, 1985.

115

Szasz, T. *Sex by Prescription*. Garden City, N.Y.: Anchor Press/Doubleday, 1980.

Williams, P. *Coming*. Glen Allen, Calif.: Entwhistle Books, 1977.

Zilbergeld, B. *Male Sexuality*. Boston: Little, Brown, 1978.

Chapter 2

Gannon, L. "The Psychophysiology of Psychosomatic Disorders." In Haynes, B. and Gannon, L. (eds.), *Psychosomatic Disorders*. New York: Praeger, 1981.

Lowen, A. *Love and Organism*. New York: Macmillan, 1965.

Mann, W., and Hoffman, E. *The Man Who Dreamed of Tomorrow: A Conceptual Biography of Wilhelm Reich*. Los Angeles: J. P. Tarcher, 1980.

Reich, W. *The Function of the Orgasm*. New York: Simon and Schuster, 1973.

Saeger, L. "The Historical Development of Bioenergetic Concepts: A Foundation for the Emerging Technology of Psycho-Physiological Therapeutics." In Cassius, J. (ed.), *Horizons in Bioenergetics*. Memphis: Promethean, 1980.

Smith, E. "Seven Decision Points." *Voices*, 1979, 15, 3, 45–50.

_____. *The Body in Psychotherapy*. Jefferson, N.C.: McFarland, 1985.

_____. "Retroflection: The Forms of Non-Enactment." *The Gestalt Journal*, 1986, 9, 1, 36–54.

Chapter 3

Gannon, L. "The Psychophysiology of Psychosomatic Disorders." In Haynes, B. and Gannon, L. (eds.), *Psychosomatic Disorders*. New York: Praeger, 1981.

Heiman, J., and Hatch, J. "Conceptual and Therapeutic Contributions of Psychophysiology to Sexual Dysfunction." In Haynes, S., and Gannon, L. (eds.), *Psychosomatic Disorders*. New York: Praeger, 1981.

Kaplan, H. *The New Sex Therapy*. New York: Brunner/Mazel, 1974.

Polster, E., and Polster, M. *Gestalt Therapy Integrated*. New York: Brunner/Mazel, 1973.

Reich, W. *The Function of the Orgasm*. New York: Touchstone, 1973.

Saeger, L. "The Historical Development of Bioenergetic Concepts: A Foundation for the Emerging Technology of Psycho-Physiological Therapeutics." In Cassius, J. (ed.), *Horizons in Bioenergetics*. Memphis: Promethean, 1980.

Smith, E. "Seven Decision Points." *Voices*, 1979, 15, 3, 45–50.

_____. *The Body in Psychotherapy*. Jefferson, N.C.: McFarland, 1985.

Steen, E., and Montagu, A. *Anatomy and Physiology*, volume II. New York: Barnes and Noble, 1959.

Wolpe, J. *Psychotherapy and Reciprocal Inhibition*. Stanford, Calif.: Stanford University Press, 1958.

Chapter 4

Lowen, A. *Breathing, Movement, and Feeling* (published lectures). New York: Institute for Bioenergetic Analysis, 1965.

Offit, A. *Night Thoughts: Reflections of a Sex Therapist*. New York: Congdon and Lattès, 1981.

Perls, F. *Ego, Hunger and Aggression*. New York: Vintage, 1969.

_____, Hefferline, R., and Goodman, P. *Gestalt Therapy: Excitement and Growth in the Human Personality*. New York: Dell, 1951.

Reich, W. *Genitality in the Theory and Therapy of Neurosis*. New York: Farrar, Straus, and Giroux, 1980.

_____. *The Function of the Orgasm*. New York: Touchstone, 1973.

Steen, E., and Montagu, A. *Anatomy and Physiology*, volume II. New York: Barnes and Noble, 1959.

Chapter 5

Enright, J. "An Introduction to Gestalt Techniques." In Fagan, J., and Shepherd, I. (eds.), *Gestalt Therapy Now*. Palo Alto, Calif.: Science and Behavior Books, 1970.

Freud, S. "The Most Prevalent Form of Degradation in Erotic Life." In Rieff, P. (ed.), *The Collected Papers of Sigmund Freud*. New York: Collier Books, 1963.

Perls, F. *Ego, Hunger and Aggression*. New York: Vintage, 1969.

_____. *The Gestalt Approach and Eye Witness to Therapy*. Palo Alto, Calif.: Science and Behavior Books, 1973.

_____. *Legacy from Fritz*. Palo Alto, Calif.: Science and Behavior Books, 1975.

_____, Hefferline, R., and Goodman, P. *Gestalt Therapy: Excitement and Growth in the Human Personality*. New York: Dell, 1951.

Polster, E., and Polster, M. *Gestalt Therapy Integrated*. New York: Brunner/Mazel, 1973.

Chapter 6

Baumgardner, P. *Gifts from Lake Cowichan*. Palo Alto, Calif.: Science and Behavior Books, 1975.

Enright, J. "An Introduction to Gestalt Techniques." In Fagan, J. and Shepherd, I. (eds.), *Gestalt Therapy Now*. Palo Alto, Calif.: Science and Behavior Books, 1970.

Perls, F. *Ego, Hunger and Aggression*. New York: Vintage, 1969.

_____. *In and Out the Garbage Pail*. Lafayette, Calif.: Real People Press, 1969.

_____, Hefferline, R., and Goodman, P. *Gestalt Therapy: Excitement and Growth in the Human Personality*. New York: Dell, 1951.

Reich, W. *Character Analysis*. New York: Noonday Press, 1949.

_____. *The Cancer Biopathy*. New York: Farrar, Straus and Giroux, 1973.

Smith, E. *The Body in Psychotherapy*. Jefferson, N.C.: McFarland, 1985.

Zinker, J. *Creative Process in Gestalt Therapy*. New York: Brunner/Mazel, 1977.

Chapter 7

Hamilton, E. *Mythology*. New York: Mentor, 1942.

Offit, A. *Night Thoughts: Reflections of a Sex Therapist*. New York: Congdon and Lattès, 1981.

Perls, F., Hefferline, R., and Goodman, P. *Gestalt Therapy: Excitement and Growth in the Human Personality*. New York: Dell, 1951.

Polster, E., and Polster, M. *Gestalt Therapy Integrated*. New York: Brunner/Mazel, 1973.

Smith, E. *The Body in Psychotherapy*. Jefferson, N.C.: McFarland, 1985.

Zinker, J. *Creative Process in Gestalt Therapy*. New York: Brunner/Mazel, 1977.

Chapter 8

Allen, C. "Perversions, Sexual." In Ellis, A., and Abarbanel, A. (eds.), *The Encyclopedia of Sexual Behavior*. New York: Hawthorn Books, 1961.

Baker, E. *Man in the Trap*. New York: Collier, 1967.

Kaplan, H. *The New Sex Therapy*. New York: Brunner/Mazel, 1974.

Karpman, B. *The Sexual Offender and His Offenses*. New York: Julian Press, 1962.

Keleman, S. *In Defense of Heterosexuality*. Berkeley, Calif.: Center Press, 1982.

Reich, W. *The Function of the Orgasm*. New York: Simon and Schuster, 1973.

Reiff, P. (ed.). *Freud: General Psychological Theory*. New York: Collier, 1963.

Rothgeb, C. *Abstracts of the Standard Edition of the Complete Psychological Works of Sigmund Freud*. New York: Jason Aronson, 1973.

Rycroft, C. *A Critical Dictionary of Psychoanalysis*. New York: Basic Books, 1968.
Stoller, R. *Sex and Gender*. New York: Science House, 1968.

Chapter 9

Barker–Benefield, G. "The Spermatic Economy: A Nineteenth–Century View of Sexuality." In Altherr, T. (ed.), *Procreation or Pleasure?: Sexual Attitudes in American History*. Malabar, Fl.: Robert E. Krieger, 1983.
Cott, N. "Passionlessness: An Interpretation of Victorian Sexual Ideology, 1790–1850." In Altherr, T. (ed.), *Procreatio or Pleasure?: Sexual Attitudes in American History*. Malabar, Fl.: Robert E. Krieger, 1983.
Goodman, P. *Nature Heals: Psychological Essays*. New York: Free Life Editions, 1977.
Haller, J. "From Maidenhood to Menopause: Sex Education for Women in Victorian America." In Altherr, T. (ed.), *Procreation or Pleasure?: Sexual Attitudes in American History*. Malabar, Fl.: Robert E. Krieger, 1983.
Keleman, S. *In Defense of Heterosexuality*. Berkeley, Calif.: Center Press, 1982.
Lowen, A. *Sex and Personality*. New York: Institute of Bioenergetic Analysis, 1963.
Mann, W., and Hoffman, E. *The Man Who Dreamed of Tomorrow*. Los Angeles: Tarcher, 1980.
Moranty, R. "The Scientist as Sex Crusader: Alfred C. Kinsey and the American Culture." In Altherr, T. (ed.), *Procreation or Pleasure?: Sexual Attitudes in American History*. Malabar, Fl.: Robert E. Krieger, 1983.
Morgan, E. "The Puritans and Sex." In Altherr, T. (ed.), *Procreation or Pleasure?: Sexual Attitudes in American History*. Malabar, Fl.: Robert E. Krieger, 1983.
Perls, F., Hefferline, R., and Goodman, P. *Gestalt Therapy*. New York: Dell, 1951.
Reich, W. *The Sexual Revolution*. New York: Farrar, Straus and Giroux, 1969.
————. *The Function of the Orgasm*. New York: Simon and Schuster, 1973.
————. *Genitality in the Theory and Therapy of Neurosis*. New York: Farrar, Straus, Giroux, 1980.
Strong, B. "Ideas of the Early Sex Education Movement in America, 1890–1920." In Altherr, T. (ed.), *Procreation or Pleasure?: Sexual Attitudes in American History*. Malabar, Fl.: Robert E. Krieger, 1983.
Szasz, T. *Sex by Prescription*. New York: Anchor Press/Doubleday, 1980.

Index

Abarbanel, A. 88
Aberration of aim 87, 88
Aberration of object 87, 88
Abstinence, sexual 9, 13–18, 114
Abuse, self 1
Abuse, sexual 93
Action 24, 25, 35, 40, 41, 45, 60, 63, 64, 66, 67, 72, 77, 89, 90, 96, 97, 113
Action/interaction–perverted SCWC 91, 97
Action–interaction sequence 94, 100
Action–interaction, sexual 26, 80, 90
Action–perverted SCWC 91
Action, retroflection of 63, 64, 66–72, 74, 76, 83, 100
Activity, sexual 6, 7, 80

Adam, M. 20, 23
Alcohol 49, 50
Alienation, self 33
Aliveness 1–3, 23
Aliveness, sexual 1, 4, 6, 7, 10, 18, 37, 50, 76, 91, 101, 114
Allen, Clifford 88, 90, 97
Alternatives 5
American sexuality 101–107, 113
Anatomical extensions 86
ANS 30, 35, 41
Anxiety 4, 29, 43, 48
Anxious contraction 29, 41
Archetype 81
Armor, body 64, 71, 72, 74, 100
Armor, muscular 69
Arousal 24, 25, 27, 34, 35, 40, 41, 45, 46, 51, 52, 59, 61, 89, 91, 111–113

Revolution, sexual 112
Rhythm, Contact/withdrawal 27, 29
Rhythms, sexual 16, 24, 31, 33, 37, 40, 41, 60, 101, 109
Rothgeb, C. 85, 86
Rush, Benjamin 2
Rycroft, C. 86

Saeger, Louis 30, 41
SANS 30, 41, 42
Satisfaction 7, 25–27, 29, 35, 40, 41, 53, 59, 60, 75, 85, 89, 94, 110–113
Scoptophilia 97
Script, platonic 58
Script, sexual 39–41
SCWC 23–27, 29, 31, 33–35, 39, 41, 43–46, 48, 49, 51–54, 56, 57, 59–62, 64, 66, 72, 75–78, 83, 89–91, 94, 95, 97, 99, 100, 112; action/interaction–perverted 91, 97; action–perverted 91; interaction–perverted 91; perverted 95, 97, 100
Self: abuse 1; alienation 33; control 64; discipline 64; exploration 3; interruption 33–35, 37, 39–41, 45, 46, 53, 56, 61, 63–66, 72, 75, 78, 80, 99, 100; knowing 3; love 80, 81; relating 1, 77
Sensuality 27, 58, 113
Sex education 114
Sex-negative society 109–111
Sex-positive society 112
Sex therapy 106
Sexology 105, 107
Sexual: abstinence 9, 13–18; abuse 93; action–interaction 26, 80, 90; activity 6, 7, 80; aliveness 1,

4, 6, 7, 10, 18, 37, 50, 76, 91, 101, 114; arousal 7, 25, 45, 48–50, 83, 91, 111–113; deadening 45, 53, 63, 75, 83, 99, 114; deviations 83, 85; dysfunction 7, 43, 83, 99; emotion 25; energy 45; expansion 71; expression 25, 26, 102, 108, 113; interaction 77, 78, 80; morals 101–105; need 25, 34, 89; perversion 83, 85–87, 90, 91, 93, 95, 99–101, 113; pleasure 91, 93, 105, 108; preference 24, 25, 34, 91, 94, 97, 113, 114; psychopathology 33, 99; responsibility 108, 109; revolution 112; rhythms 16, 24, 31, 33, 37, 40, 41, 60, 101, 109; satisfaction 6, 7, 75, 108, 110–113; self-alienation 33; self-interruption 33–35, 37, 39, 40; tension 1, 8, 9, 13, 85, 89, 99–102; urge 108–110; violence 113, 114; want 26, 29, 34, 89; withdrawal 45, 110
Sexual attitudes, American 101–107, 113; Catholic 102, 103; moral 87, 88, 101, 102, 105, 108; political 87, 88, 101, 107, 109, 111; puritan 102, 103; religious 87, 102; Victorian 103–105, 109; sexological 105, 107
Sexual Contact/Withdrawal Cycle (see SCWC)
Sexual script 39–41
Sexual script, toxic 52, 58–60, 65, 100, 109
Sexuality 27, 59, 66, 83, 91, 101, 102, 107, 110, 113, 114; American 101–107, 113; deadened 83, 114; perverse 83, 113; purposes 91; violent 113, 114